Preface

For teachers, the use of ICT is increasingly important, both for their work with children in the classroom and for other aspects of their professional work. It provides enormous possibilities for raising standards in education and for facilitating the teacher's work. The only question is that of how best to learn how to use ICT. Teachers know that everyone learns in ways that suit their own abilities. They also know that learning with a particular purpose is likely to be more effective than learning without one. Learning with a purpose is the premise that has driven the organisation and content of this series of books. The result aims to be a set of resources that teachers will find to be practical, effective and above all, written with the specific needs of teachers in mind.

Each book has a focus on one aspect of work with ICT. There are six sections in each book. Section 1 gives an overview of how ICT can help with the work and some basics relating to the ICT applications that are most appropriate to use. Sections 2-5 all start with a question about how ICT can help with a typical activity a teacher might want to do. The sections then describe the ICT techniques that teachers can use to do the activities. Section 6 shows how ICT work can be planned and gives examples of how the techniques can be used in the classroom.

The techniques described apply to a wide range of different programs. There are step-by-step instructions that relate to specific programs. The authors have chosen to use the **Office '97** suite of programs as a generic core with other programs chosen to illustrate what can be done. Although this is a realistic choice based on what is available in most schools and is used by most teachers, it cannot cater for every requirement. Nor can the techniques aim to include every way of carrying out an activity. Usually, there are alternative ways to do the same procedures, some of which may be faster.

A number of worked examples of classroom activities is provided. The focus of these however, is not intended to be on the subject but on ways in which the techniques can be used. Unlike subject-focused ICT training, the authors believe that teachers will be able to apply and adapt ideas to their own subject teaching and other needs. The techniques to research, to compose, to handle data or to present information are largely the same, irrespective of the subject context. For teachers of Key Stage 1 and 2, there is little point in learning the same techniques in the context of every National Curriculum subject. In a secondary school, specialist teachers can extend their knowledge of ICT by developing a greater understanding of work in other subjects.

Working with ICT involves experimenting, making mistakes, finding your own ways to do tasks and applying what you learn to new situations. At times, you may find it frustrating for reasons that are beyond your control. We hope you can enjoy the learning experience.

Emma Asprey
Fred Martin
Andy Weymouth
Bath Spa University College

Contents

Introduction to exchanging and sharing information

Book aims

This book has two main aims.
- To help teachers use the multimedia features of ICT to present ideas so that they can create teaching and learning resources for children.
- To show how the multimedia features of ICT can be related to work that children need to do to achieve standards for National Curriculum Orders in different subjects.

Many of these techniques can also be used to help teachers with other professional work such as administration and for personal development.

Compose, modify and design

The process of creating teaching and learning resources has several phases. The first phase—researching information—is the focus for a separate book in this series (*Click on ... Searching*). Using the information, a basic presentation can then be planned and created. The text may need to be edited and pictures and layout altered, both for accuracy and suitability for audience. By this stage, the content should read well and contain ideas that need to be taught and learnt, but to create a resource that works effectively and looks good, further design work must be done. Although first rate content is essential, this is only of limited value if it is difficult for children to read and uninspiring for them to look at. The techniques described in this book aim to help make the resources both accessible and inviting to your audiences.

The value of ICT

Few teachers have the gift to produce hand written resources that are attractive and well designed. Used properly, ICT can be a powerful tool to achieve professional results. Many ICT techniques are relatively basic and are available to everyone from the start. It is then only time and regular use which increases knowledge, competence and confidence.

Some of the ways that ICT can help to create resources are to:
- show initial ideas on screen in a way that remain open to change
- enable you to include different types of resources such as diagrams, photos, sound and video as well as text
- edit text and other resources quickly, selectively and cleanly
- enable modification of a resource to help achieve differentiation
- make interactive resources which can be presented to children or used by them independently.

Be your own publisher

An additional advantage of ICT is that it gives you control over most of the phases of producing resources. You can write resources specifically for the children you teach instead of relying on commercial products that may not be entirely suitable. This of course, can be a mixed blessing as it means you have to do all the work. The result however, is more likely to be one that is most effective for your audience.

? Think *about*

- Look at some resources you have produced recently. What techniques do you use now to make your resources look inviting and make them easy for children to access and use?

- Are there any features you cannot, but would like to use? As an example, think about how you might use multimedia.

- What is the process you use now to produce resources and in what order do you take the individual steps in the process?

ICT applications

The power of multimedia

The main focus in this book is on the techniques to create multimedia publications. There is a wide range of software available that you can use to create your own resources.

The techniques extend into:
- collect and use of a variety of different types of resource such as photographs, diagrams, clip art, video and sound
- use of design features such as backgrounds, layout, transitions and links
- use of colour for text, images, design features and backgrounds
- interactive features such as creating links between pages and hyperlinks to the Internet
- page layouts and presentation structure
- linking ICT applications to create effective on-screen and hard copy resources
- sending images, sounds and files via email.

Multimedia authoring programs

Different multimedia authoring programs have different tools and functions, though most share a broad range of common features. The techniques described in this book refer to what can be done with Digital Workshop's *Illuminatus 4.5* multimedia authoring package. Many of the techniques can also be used with earlier versions of *Illuminatus* and with other multimedia authoring packages. Some techniques cannot. Although *Illuminatus 4.5* may not be the most recent version of *Illuminatus*, it has enough tools and functions to make it a powerful tool to create resources. A general principle however, is to plan to update to the most recent software, especially when new and useful tools become available.

There is a range of multimedia authoring software available. The most commonly found in schools are *Illuminatus (Digital Workshop)* and *Hyperstudio (Tag)*. This type of software allows you to create multimedia publications which can be used as presentations or can be explored by other users. The result can resemble an adventure game, talking story, encyclopaedia or web site. Other packages available include *Textease Multimedia (Softease)*, *Adobe Premier (Adobe)* and *Corel Click & Create (Corel)*.

Some multimedia authoring packages that aim to be child-friendly have a limited range of tools and functions. They usually also have enlarged text commands and icons. There are some advantages in using these programs, especially with the very youngest children and when children are creating their own work.

There are however, considerable restrictions on the types of resources and activities that you can create if only these basic programs are available both to you and the children. The children's own progress in the use of ICT may also be held back.

Teachers need to carefully weigh up the advantages and disadvantages of these limited range programs. A useful compromise option is to be able to choose a level at which to work.

? Think *about*

- What multimedia authoring software do the children you teach have access to when they are in school?

- For children with a computer at home, find out if they have any multimedia authoring software available.

- If the children you teach only use basic software in school, are you certain that this is all they would be able to use and are you clear about why this choice has been made?

Presentation software

An alternative to using a multimedia authoring package for creating resources is to use a presentation program. Some of the techniques are the same and at least some of the commands and tools are similar, though there are also some key differences in how some of the functions work. The most important difference is that presentation programs are designed to create linear presentations, whereas multimedia authoring software is designed to produce open-ended packages to be used by a wider audience. In spite of these differences, many of the ideas in this book can be applied equally to both types of program. You will need to decide which type of program you want to use to create your resources.

The most commonly used presentation software is **Microsoft PowerPoint**. This allows you to create an electronic slide show using text, images, sound, animation and special effects. Other packages available include **Project Presenter (Semerc)** and **Internet Odyssey (Granada Learning)**.

Web publishing software

Web publishing software allows you to create web sites incorporating many features of multimedia authoring software plus maintenance and management features. There is a wide range of software available including **FrontPage (Microsoft)**, **Dreamweaver (Macromedia)**, **Page Mill (Adobe)**, and **Hot Dog Junior (RM)**.

Email

Email can be accessed using software such as **Outlook Express (Microsoft)** or **Netscape Messenger (Netscape)**. This is usually an account which can only be accessed from one machine or network using your Internet Service Provider (ISP).

Other generic programs

Some of the tools in a word processor can achieve similar results to a multimedia authoring program. However, a word processor was not designed to do this job fully and easily. The ideal position to be in is one in which you have a choice of the type of software you want to use and the knowledge of what it can do .

Linking ICT

Creating resources often involves using more than one type of program, even if the resource itself is written with a multimedia authoring package. Images can be captured using a digital camera or scanner then processed using graphics software. Images can also be copied and inserted from a CD-ROM or from the Internet. Sounds can be recorded and processed using media players.

One key to using ICT successfully is being able to move quickly between different types of program. This can be to copy and paste resources and to use the functions that each type of program does best. Encouraging children to work in the same way will help them to develop their ICT capabilities to a much higher level than working with only one type of program at a time.

K Key *words*

digital camera: a camera that takes photos in digital form

generic program: a program that does not have its own subject content so that you can use it to create your own work

scanner: a copier that captures pictures in digital form that can be used in a computer

? Think *about*

■ What generic programs do the children you teach use when they are in school?

■ Why do you think it can be an advantage for you to have different types of generic programs with which you can create your own resources?

■ Why might it be an advantage to be able to use several different types of program to create resources?

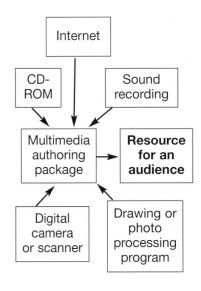

Ways of working

The activities described in this book provide opportunities for children to work individually, in groups or in the whole class. This raises challenges that are common to all curriculum subjects and there are many advantages to a flexible approach to the organisation and grouping of children.

Individual work

When children work at computers on their own, it is easier to assess what progress has been made by the individual, although few schools have access to facilities which allow each child to work at their own computer. There are many practical and logistical reasons why individual work is rarely possible.

Group work

Paired or group work can encourage interaction and collaboration between children, although this will not happen automatically and requires careful management and organisation. If a computer suite is available, it may still be desirable for children to work in groups for many activities. When organising the grouping there are several issues to consider:

- **Learning Objectives**
  Consider whether the use of ICT is the best method of achieving the objectives for the lesson. Ensure that the activity is purposeful and placed within the context of the subject work going on in the classroom. If the development of collaborative or social skills is one of the learning objectives, this needs to be made clear to the children.
- **Children's Learning**
  Children's IT and subject capabilities need to be considered, as do the personalities involved. Avoid domination of control over the equipment or ideas by selecting pairs or groups carefully. Grouping can be used to provide differentiated activities to meet the needs of all children, just as in any other subject work.
- **Teaching**
  Consider how much support particular pairs or groups will need. This may depend on the method of introducing the activity. It may be sensible to make use of other adults in the classroom to support children, and careful use of peer tutoring could be appropriate for some groups and activities. Peer support can increase confidence and independent working when well managed.

Whole class teaching

Whole class teaching of ICT is possible with one computer in a classroom, especially where a teacher is able to model skills using a data projector, large TV or monitor. Whole class use of ICT is only possible using a suite of computers or a class set of laptops. It is necessary in both cases for all the computers to be running the same software and systems, ideally using a network. This can be valuable and allow children to support each other when applying the skills to subject-based work. Whole class work can allow children to share ideas and information and allow you to reinforce teaching points and discuss the challenges encountered during a lesson.

Teaching and learning

Developing and communicating ideas

Much of teaching and learning has always been about how to develop and present ideas and this now been built into National Curriculum work across all subjects. ICT is also an essential part of work in all subjects. Using ICT to help develop and present ideas provides a link between these two demands.

NC subject Orders

In some subjects, the National Curriculum Orders include specific references to using ICT for information research, often as part of sections in the Programmes of Study that relate to subject skills. In others, there is a broader requirement to ensure that ICT is used.

The NC Orders for ICT

The NC Orders for ICT include statements at both KS 1 and KS 2 that require children to develop their ideas on-screen and to be able to modify what they have written (see the table below).

ICT standards for teachers

There are also new standards in ICT that teachers must achieve and these are set out in two documents:
- Annex B to DfEE Circular 4/98 sets out the ICT standards to achieve qualified teacher status (QTS).
- Annex A1 (England, Wales and Northern Ireland) and Annex A2 (Scotland) in the 'Use of ICT in subject teaching – NOF-funded training – Expected outcomes for teachers'.

These documents use the term 'capacity and range' to describe the amount and variety of forms of information that ICT can handle (Annex A, 14 b). The word 'provisionality' is used to describe how work can be changed and alternatives explored.

ICT for teachers

New Opportunities Fund (NOF) ICT training for teachers is based on the same ICT standards that are required of all trainee teachers. The standards for NOF training are listed in Annex A

The standards for trainee teachers are listed in Annex B to DfEE Circular 4/98.

Key Stage 1

2 Developing ideas and making things happen
a use text, tables, images and sound to develop their ideas

3 Exchanging and sharing information
a how to share their ideas by presenting information in a variety of forms
b to present their completed work effectively

4 Reviewing, modifying and evaluating work as it progresses
a review what they have done to help them develop their ideas
c talk about what they might change in future work

Key Stage 2

2 Developing ideas and making things happen
a how to develop and refine ideas by bringing together, organising and reorganising text, tables, images and sound as appropriate

3 Exchanging and sharing information
a how to share information in a variety of ways
b to be sensitive to the needs of the audience and think carefully about the content and quality when communicating information

4 Reviewing, modifying and evaluating work as it progresses
a review what they and others have done to help them develop their ideas
b describe and talk about the effectiveness of their work with ICT, comparing it with other methods and considering the effect it has had on others
c talk about how they could improve future work

Planning

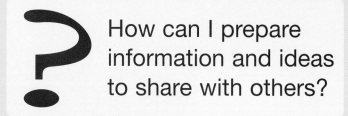

How can I prepare information and ideas to share with others?

K Key *words*

Presentation: an electronic slide show

Multimedia package: software that can show sound, images, text, video and animation with buttons to link different resources

Web site: a series of linked pages of information on the Internet

CD-ROM: a CD containing multimedia information which can be accessed but not altered

Bullet point: a mark to show one item in a list

Try *this*

■ Produce a flow chart to plan the creation of an interactive big book to use in a Literacy lesson. Make sure you have a clear picture of what you want to create.

■ Take the content of a topic to be taught to your class next term.

■ Spilt it into 4 sections, each with 3/4 bullet points.

■ Summarise the content of your medium-term planning using the headings you have chosen.

How it works

Good **presentations**, **multimedia packages** and **web sites** must be thoroughly thought out and planned. Because the software is easy to use, it is tempting to plunge in and start without preparation. There are several issues to consider:

● What is the reason for creating the presentation, multimedia package or web site?
● Who will the audience be?
● How will you make your work distinctive?
● Which resources will you need?
● Where will the resources come from?

You should produce a flow chart to answer the questions above, before you start creating your presentation, multimedia package or web site. You will then need to collect resources and organise them effectively. You may also wish to decide on the structure, fonts, backgrounds and layouts to be used. Links between sections or pages need to be mapped out to ensure there is a sensible overall structure.

The techniques

Deciding on the content

Once you have decided that a multimedia presentation or **web site** is the most effective way to communicate your information or ideas, you then need to make choices about what to include. It is always helpful to look at other resources which have been produced on the same subject. Explore a **CD-ROM** or look at some web sites to inform your decisions about what to include.

Once you have decided on the content of the publication, split it into pages or slides. This will help you to summarise the information you want to include. If you are producing a presentation you should use **bullet points** rather than include every detail on the slides. Think of them as prompt cards rather than an essay.

Consider the best way of presenting the information and ideas. You will need to decide when it is best to use text, images, video, music and sound effects. Take into account the audience and purpose of the publication.

Creating a structure

Once you have decided on the content of your publication, you need to create a structure to work within. This will include the way in which the information is presented and broken into sections. You will also need to consider how the information is ordered and linked together.

A multimedia presentation can be a simple **linear structure**. A multimedia publication or web site can be much more complex, using a **hierarchical structure**. Any buttons linking different sections of the publication or **hyperlinks** to other web sites will need to be planned to ensure correct sections are linked and everything is included.

You should also look at the structure of the whole publication and make some decisions about the amount and nature of images, video and sound files to be used. You will need to decide when multimedia elements can be used to enhance the resource and when they cause a distraction from the educational content. Children will also need to learn to use these features appropriately. Multimedia features should be used to suit the audience and purpose of the publication rather than for the amusement of the author.

At every stage of planning, consider the audience and purpose of the publication. Keep this at the centre of your thoughts to ensure that the content is the focus rather than the special effects which can distract the audience instead of helping them to concentrate.

K Key *words*

Linear structure: a structure in which events happen in a predetermined order in sequence

Hierarchical structure: a structure in which information is organised into sections which can be explored as the user wishes

Hyperlink: a link between different marked places in a document or between documents

Try *this*

■ Using the presentation you created to summarise your planning, add planned links to useful web sites for each section. These might be to use with children or for colleagues to use.

■ Plan links to other useful documents, such as cross-curricular planning, display ideas and resource sheets.

Slide 1
Title
Author
Visual & sound effect

Slide 2
Title
Introduction to presentation
Visual effects on bullet points
Image?

Slide 3
Title
Section 1
Detail
Visual effects on bullet points
Image

Slide 4
Title
Section 2
Detail
Visual effects on bullet points
Image

Slide 5
Title
Section 3
Detail
Visual effects on bullet points
Image

Slide 6
Title
Section 4
Detail
Visual effects on bullet points
Image

Slide 7
Title
Conclusion
Visual effects on bullet points
Image

Starting from scratch

If you have never presented information or ideas using multimedia before, a presentation is the simplest form to use. Presentation software can be used to produce linear presentations, like electronic slide shows. Each new **slide** appears when you click the mouse.

Microsoft PowerPoint is the most commonly used presentation software. It allows you to use text, images, animations and sound effects to present ideas and information.

The process of producing and using a presentation can be helpful in structuring ideas and communicating them in a suitable way. This can benefit teachers and children.

Creating a new presentation

To create a new presentation using ***Microsoft PowerPoint***, double click on the icon on the desktop. You will be given the options of using a **wizard**, **template** or blank presentation. Choosing to work on a blank presentation allows you explore all the available tools.

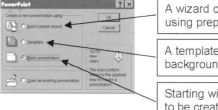

A wizard can be used to create publications using prepared styles and colours.

A template can be used to provide a background scheme and font style.

Starting with a blank presentation allows you to be creative and produce individual work.

Choosing a layout

You will then be given the choice of a variety of **slide layouts**. Each slide is like a page in a book, each can be different but they will be saved as one file. There are layouts suitable for titles, bullet pointed lists, images, tables, charts, graphs and video clips. Whichever you choose, it can be altered at any time to include other elements and features.

🔲 Key *words*

Slide: one page within a presentation

Slide layout: the positioning of text, images, charts and tables on a slide

Wizard: a process in which you answer a sequence of questions in order to produce a document

Template: a page design provided as part of the program

❗ Teaching *idea: English*

Planning a presentation involves the development of speaking and listening skills, as well as reading from different sources and writing in a concise form, taking account of audience.

👆 Try *this*

- Start *PowerPoint* by double clicking on the icon on the desktop.

- Familiarise yourself with the buttons on the toolbar. You will notice that many of them are the same as those encountered when word processing or using a spreadsheet.

- Explore the wizards and templates.

Adding text

When you select a suitable layout, the slide will contain brief instructions about how to enter information onto it. Text is automatically bullet pointed. To switch off the bullets, click once in the frame and click on the **bullet point** button on the toolbar.

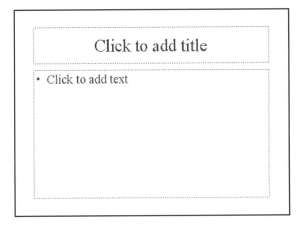

*A **PowerPoint** slide containing text frames for a title and bullet pointed list.*

Changing frames

Enter the information into the frames as required. To change the size of any of the frames, click once in the frame so that the border appears. Resize the frame by clicking and dragging from any of the corner or side points using the double ended arrow.

To move the frame, put the pointer in the middle of the active frame and click and drag using the four-pointed arrow.

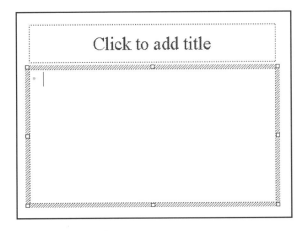

*A **PowerPoint** slide in which the text frame is active. It can now be resized or moved.*

Animating elements

Bullet points can be animated so that each appears on the screen at the click of the mouse. This enables the presenter to control the pace of the presentation and helps the audience to concentrate on the current point being made.

Pictures, charts, graphs and other elements can also be animated. This means that they can be made to appear at the appropriate time to illustrate a point rather than detract from it.

 Try *this*

■ Type a title into the title frame

■ Type a list into the main text frame

■ Alter the size and/or position of the title and text frames

Click on the text or image to be animated.
Select **Custom Animation** from the **Slide Show** menu.

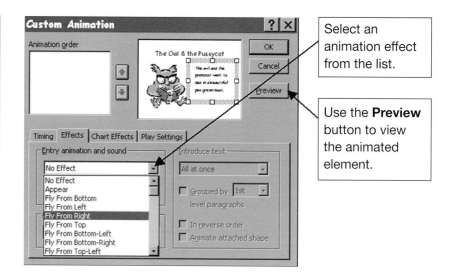

Select an animation effect from the list.

Use the **Preview** button to view the animated element.

You can animate any element on your slide. Make sure you click on the element before selecting **Custom Animation** from the **Slide Show** menu.

Adding slides

To insert a new slide in your presentation, click on the **New Slide** button on the toolbar.

Think of each slide like a new slide. When you save your work, you will automatically save all the slides together as one document.

To view slides use the vertical **scrollbar** to move backwards and forwards through the slides.

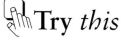

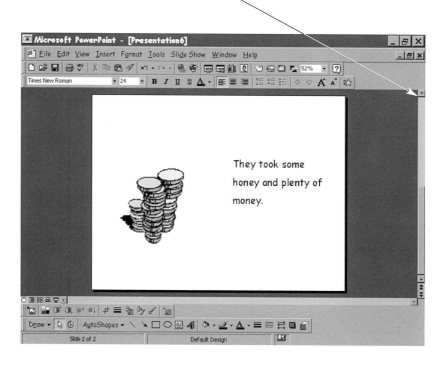

K Key *words*

Custom animation: visual and sound effects added to text and images

Scrollbar: the side bar tool to move through a document

Slide Show: view in which slide show is actively running and cannot be edited

Try *this*

■ Animate a bullet pointed list to make each item appear on the screen at the click of the mouse

■ Animate an image and add a sound effect

Views

Once you have created a series of slides, you can view them in several different ways, each of which has its uses.

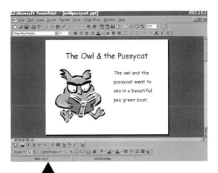

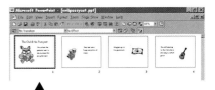

Slide View

This shows the whole slide and is best for designing layout and editing content.

Outline View

This shows you the text of each slide and a thumbnail of the whole slide. It is best used for editing the text of the whole presentation and ensuring continuity. Slide order can also be changed.

Slide Sorter View

This shows thumbnails of the whole presentation. Text and images cannot be edited, but the order of the slides can be changed and effects applied to the whole presentation.

Notes Page View

This shows a thumbnail of the slide and allows you to make accompanying notes.

Slide Show

In this view you can see and hear special effects. Each slide fills the screen. Move from one slide to the next by clicking the mouse. Run your slide show regularly to ensure your message is being communicated effectively.

Press **Escape** to return to the slide view.

🖑 Try *this*

- Make a list of points to be made at a staff meeting or to be introduced to your class.

- Split them into three sections and type them onto three slides using bullet points.

- Animate the points.

- When using the presentation with staff or pupils, you can make use of the features of the software by discussing each point in turn and stopping to edit points when necessary.

Ⓚ Key *words*

Scrollbar: the side bar tool to move through a document

Slide View: view in which the whole slide can be seen and edited

Outline View: view in which the text can be seen and edited

Slide Sorter View: view in which the order of the slides can be altered

Notes Page View: view in which presenter's notes can be written

Slide Show: view in which slide show is actively running and cannot be edited

Text and images

K Key *words*

Presentation software: software that combines text, images and sound in an electronic slide show

Web publishing software: software that can be used to create web pages and manage websites

Formatting tools: a set of tools used to alter the appearance of text and images

Word-processing: writing, editing and designing text

File handling: the ability to create folders, locate and move files around within a filing structure

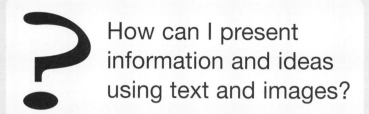

? How can I present information and ideas using text and images?

How it works

Text and images can be used to present ideas and information in imaginative and stimulating ways using presentation, multimedia authoring and web publishing software. These can be created or collected from a variety of sources, editing, resized or manipulated and used within presentations and publications.

Most software uses standard formatting tools for text and images. The skills needed are basically word-processing and some simple file handling. These are applied within software which allows a wider range of presentation tools and effects to be utilised.

*Standard and formatting toolbars in **PowerPoint**.*

*Main and formatting toolbars in **Illuminatus**.*

*Standard and formatting toolbars in **FrontPage**.*

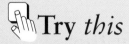 Try *this*

■ Locate any presentation, multimedia authoring or web publishing software in your school. Identify the text and image formatting tools.

■ How easy are they to use?

■ How could you use them to enhance teaching and learning in your classroom?

Generic tools

Although software may have different functions and may be produced by different companies, the menus and toolbars share many standard features. These make it easier to transfer skills and techniques, and apply them in new contexts.

Ideas and information can be shared with a wider audience, through varied presentation and electronic media, such as the Internet and email.

The techniques

Choosing a template

There are usually **templates** which can be used to save you time and assist you in making choices about appearance. This can help you to concentrate on the content rather than the cosmetics of the page.

These can usually be accessed by selecting **New** from the **File** menu.

This design will now be applied to each new slide you create.

Backgrounds

If none of these backgrounds is suitable you can create your own. Start with a blank presentation and select **Background** from the **Format** menu.

The background should be chosen to suit the content and audience. It should not detract from the content or distract the audience. Choosing a background is not just a matter of taste.

In ***Power Point***, clicking one of the icons lets you see a preview of the template.

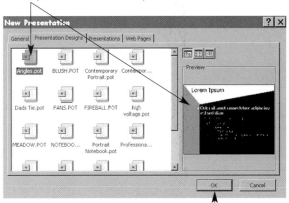

To apply the design you have chosen click on the **OK** button.

Click on **More Colours** to select a plain coloured background or **Fill Effects** for graduated colour, textures or images.

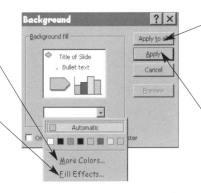

Click on **Apply to all** to place your chosen background onto every new slide.

Click on **Apply** to place it on the current slide.

There are a wide variety of styles available:

Template

Plain colour

Graduated colour

Texture

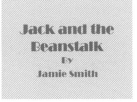

Pattern

Picture

K Key *words*

Template: a page design provided as part of the program

Graduated colour: smooth transition from one colour to another

Texture: a background image giving the effect of a texturised surface

Try *this*

■ Choose the title slide layout and add a background.

■ Experiment with different combinations of background and font style and colour.

Entering text

Depending on the software you are using, you may be able to type directly onto the page, you may need to create a text frame or there may be one already placed on the page for you to use.

Front Page *works almost like a word processor. Text is typed directly onto the page and formatted using standard tools.*

Illuminatus *requires you to create text frames using the button on the vertical* **toolbar**. *Text can then be entered and formatted using familiar tools.*

PowerPoint *provides you with templates to work in. Text frames are already placed on the pages for you. These can be resized, moved or deleted. You can create or add your own at any point.*

Formatting text

Once text has been typed in, it can be formatted in a variety of ways. The relevant tools can be found on any toolbar. To change the appearance of the text, click and drag from the beginning of the text to the end. This will **highlight** the text.

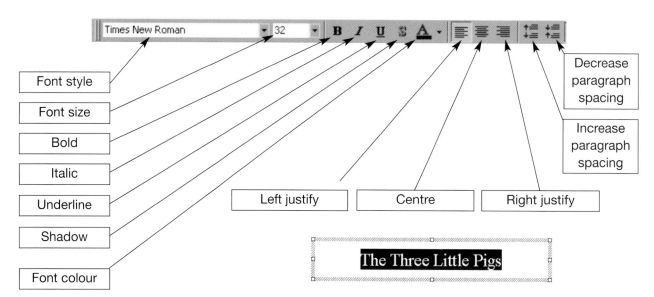

Font style

Font size

Bold

Italic

Underline

Shadow

Font colour

Decrease paragraph spacing

Increase paragraph spacing

Left justify

Centre

Right justify

Click on the appropriate button/s on the toolbar to change the **font style**, **size** or **colour** or add emphasis using **bold**, **italic**, **underline** or **shadow**. Text can be aligned to suit its purpose, for example putting a title in the centre, using the justify buttons. Spacing between paragraphs can be adjusted using the paragraph spacing buttons.

When children are formatting text, they should do so with a purpose. They need to be taught when and when not to use these tools and how to use them effectively. This should be related to the audience and purpose of the writing, rather than pure subjectivity.

Bullet points and lists

When creating presentations it can be useful to use bullet points to list the main points. To activate bullet points, click at the start of the first item and click on the bullet button on the toolbar. Each time you press the Return key a new bullet point will appear. To switch off the bullet points, click on the button again.

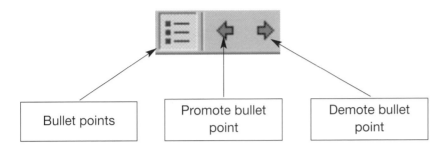

| Bullet points | Promote bullet point | Demote bullet point |

Using bullet points on a presentation slide.

Bullet points can be useful in providing a structure for a presentation. They help the audience to focus on the main points and encourage the presenter to stick to the structure, whilst elaborating on the content.

Changing bullet style

Bullet points do not have to be round dots, they can be square, dashed or a more unusual symbol. To change the style of bullet points, highlight the text and select Bullet from the Format menu.

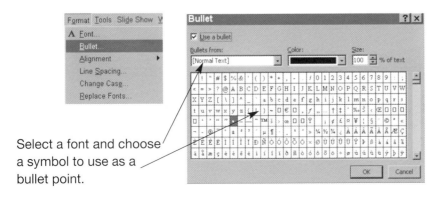

Select a font and choose a symbol to use as a bullet point.

Try *this*

- Prepare a template for children to produce a presentation by providing titles on 3 or 4 slides.

- Add 3 bullet points to each slide with suggested areas to be included.

- Change the font and background to suit the content and age of the children.

- Is there another way you could have achieved the same result?

- How will using the software enhance the children's learning?

! **Teaching** *idea: English*

Children can prepare information to be presented to two different audiences. An account of a recent event or trip could be presented to parents and younger children in the school. The content and language will need to be adapted and different fonts and organisation may be used.

Adding clip art

Clip art is a selection of images, cartoons, photographs and symbols. It often comes free with software, on free CDs with magazines or can be **downloaded** from the Internet. It is ready to use and often comes with its own **browser** to help you find pictures on any subject.

All Microsoft software comes with a good selection of clip art. The contents will vary according to which versions of software you have. The **Clip Gallery** can be used to locate a suitable image.

These images can be used by teachers to present information in more motivating ways. Children need to be taught how to use it in an appropriate manner, according to the task in hand. The purpose, size and positioning of images will need to be discussed.

Depending on the software you are using, you may be able to insert an image directly onto the page, you may need to create an **image frame** or there may be one already placed on the page for you to use.

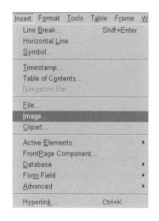

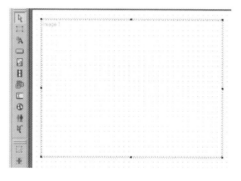

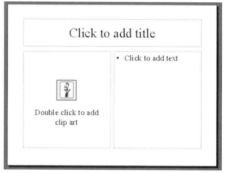

Front Page *allows you to insert an image directly onto the page using the **Insert Image** button.*

Illuminatus *requires you to create an image frame using the button on the vertical toolbar. A **dialogue box** will then appear asking you to choose an image. There is no browser to view images, so you will need to know the file name and location in advance.*

PowerPoint *provides you with image frames when you choose this type of slide layout. Double click in the image frame to activate the Clip Gallery and choose an image.*

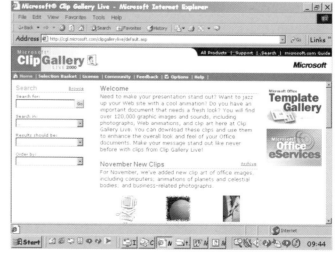

You can access thousands of images on the Microsoft web site. These can be saved or copied and pasted into documents.

The Clip Gallery

The Clip Gallery is a useful tool for finding suitable images to use with text. It will automatically start when you double click in an image frame in **Power Point**. Once an image has been inserted onto the page, it can be resized or moved to any position.

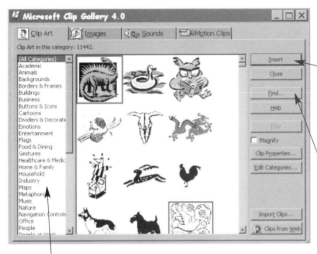

You can use the **Categories** to search through groups of images.

Click on the image you want, then click on the **Insert** button to place it on the page.

You can use the **Find** facility to look for images on a specified subject.

Use the square blocks at the corners of the image to resize it, whilst keeping the proportions correct. Your pointer will change to a double ended arrow when it is positioned correctly.

Click and drag to resize the image.

To move the image, put your pointer anywhere in the middle of the image. It will change to a four-pointed arrow.

Click and drag to reposition the image.

Try *this*

- Produce a story or poem to use during the whole class section of the Literacy hour.

- Add a suitable image onto each page to accompany the text.

- Use the resource instead of a big book during a Literacy hour. This will work most effectively if you have access to a large monitor or projector and screen.

- How does this compare with a paper-based resource?

! **Teaching** *idea:*
Design & Technology/Art

Children can examine and evaluate adverts for a range of products, these might be on paper or on television. They can analyse the types of images used for different purposes and audiences before creating their own simple advert, combining a suitable image and simple text.

Images from other sources

Before starting work on a presentation, multimedia package or web site, it is advisable to collect useful images together in a folder or on a floppy disk. Images can be collected from a variety of sources including the Internet, **digital cameras** and **scanners**. When saving images from the Internet or scanning images, ensure you stay within copyright law.

Images from the Internet

You can use a **search engine** to search for images.

By typing a subject in the search box, you can find images on almost any subject. These may include photographs, adverts, drawings, cartoons and logos. Click on an image to see it full size.

To save an image from a web site, put the pointer on the image and click the right hand mouse button. Click on **Save Picture As** on the menu. Save the image into a folder to start a collection of images on a theme.

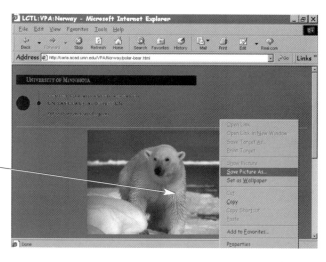

A flatbed scanner

Images from scanners

Scanners will vary in the way they work and the software they use, however the basics are the same for most models.

Place the picture you want to scan face down on the glass and close the lid. Start the scanning software from the desktop. Many scanners use Twain compatible software and will work in similar ways.

1. Check that the **Image Type** is correct.

2. **Preview** the image before you scan it.

3. Click and drag to select an area of the image if required.

4. Click on the **Scan** button.

5. Click on the **Close** button, then save using the File menu.

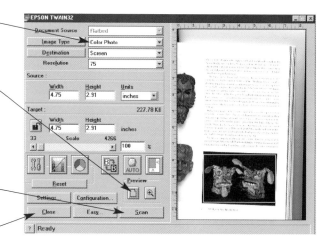

Tip

When saving image files name them *******.jpeg** This will ensure that they take up little memory and can be used in a wide range of software.

Images from digital cameras

Digital cameras can be used to obtain instant images. They are easy for children to use and can be used to record work in progress. Most digital cameras hold the images on their own internal memory. These have to be downloaded to a computer by plugging the camera into it. Some cameras use floppy disks, the images are stored on the disk and can be used immediately without the need for downloading.

As with scanned images and pictures from the Internet, it is sensible to save images on a theme together in a folder. This may mean moving them from the floppy disk to the correct location. Make sure the files have names which make them easy to use.

File formats

There are many types of graphics available and the use of the web has extended and improved these.

Vector Graphics are images created in a drawing program such as Corel Draw, Adobe Illustrator or Freehand. These images are constructed using a combination of computer commands and mathematical formulae, with images being made up of lines, circles, squares, cubes, spheres etc. These graphics can be scaled without loss of quality and can be deconstructed. Common extensions are EPS (Encapsulated Postscript) and WMF (Windows Meta File).

Raster Graphics are images created in painting programs, screen captures or by scanning/digital photography. The image is broken up into a grid, each part of which is referred to as a Picture Element or Pixel. Each pixel represents one part of the whole image, analogous to 1 tile in a mosaic. Common extensions are TIF (Tagged Image File Format) and BMP (Bitmap).

Other forms of graphics have emerged as a result of the demands of web publishing. Web graphics need to be portable and compact. The two most commonly used are GIF and JPEG.
GIF (Graphics Interchange Format) images use 256 colours or shades of grey. They can compress images to 25-10% of their original size depending on the complexity of the image. Because of the method of compression, only a little detail is lost in the process. GIFs can be given transparent backgrounds and can be animated.
JPEG (Joint Photographic Expert Group) images use up to 16.7 million colours. This uses a more complex form of compression which reduce an image to 5% of its original size. The method of compression discards detailed information, therefore the quality of an image is reduced. This format is most suitable for photographs, as the human eye is very good at filling in missing information.
PNG (Portable Network Graphic) is one of the newest forms of graphic, specially developed for use on the Internet. It has recently been endorsed by the Internet standards body, the World Wide Web Consortium (W3C).

Try *this*

■ Use the **My Computer** icon on the desktop to view image files on a floppy disk.

■ Notice what type of file each one is and how much memory it takes up.

A digital camera which saves images directly onto a floppy disk.

Tip

When you are saving graphics, always try to use a format which takes up the smallest amount of memory, whilst maintaining clarity and quality. You will need to check that the format is compatible with the software you are using to create your multimedia presentation or web site.

K Key *words*

Digital camera: a camera that takes photos in digital form

Scanner: a copier that captures pictures in digital form that can be used in a computer

Search engine: a website which facilitates searches for information on a given subject

Picture or **image toolbar:** the toolbar used to edit pictures and images

Undo: a tool to go back to a previous situation

Try *this*

■ Make a collection of images from a variety of sources on a particular topic.

■ Insert the images into a slide show to use as a stimulus for a lesson.

■ What are the advantages of using the software?

Inserting images

Whatever the source of the image, it is inserted into the presentation in exactly the same way. Click on the **Insert** menu and click on **Picture** or **Image.**

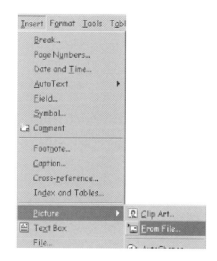

You will then need to browse to locate the file you wish to insert.

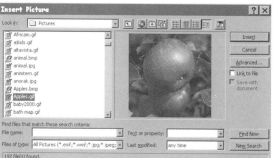

Manipulating images

Most software will allow you to alter the images once they have been inserted onto the page. If you are using *PowerPoint* or *Front Page* make sure you have the **Picture** or **Image toolbar** switched on.

The **Picture toolbar** allows you to manipulate the size, colour and appearance of the image. Click on the image, then use the buttons to alter it. You can always use the **Undo** button, if you don't like the result.

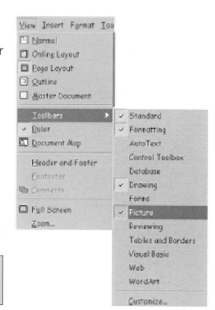

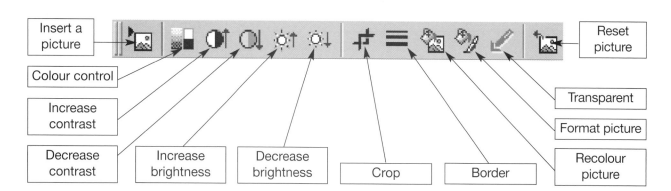

Insert a picture

Colour control

Increase contrast

Decrease contrast

Increase brightness

Decrease brightness

Crop

Border

Reset picture

Transparent

Format picture

Recolour picture

Sending text and images via email

Email enables you to communicate cheaply and quickly with people all over the world. Text can be sent very simply, using a plain email message.

Type the recipient's **email address** in the **To** box. Make sure you type it accurately and don't use any spaces.

Type a heading in the **Subject** box. This acts like a title, letting the recipient know what the message is about.

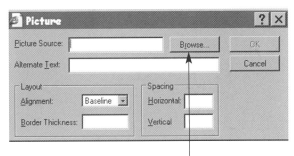

Type your message in the main screen area.

Click on **Send** to send your message.

Use the **spell check** facility

Images can be sent via email. They take up more memory than a text message and may take longer to download. It is best to avoid sending large images or those which take up a lot of memory, such as bitmaps. Most images obtained with a scanner or digital camera will automatically be in a suitable format.

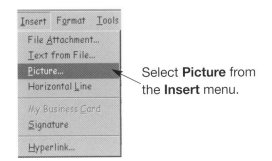

Select **Picture** from the **Insert** menu.

Browse to select the picture file you wish to insert into the message. Click **OK** to place the image in the message.

Replying to a message

Click on **Get Message** to receive the message from your colleague. Read the message in the bottom half of the screen.

To reply to the message click on the **Reply** button on the toolbar.

The computer will automatically insert the sender's address in the **To** box. All you need to do is type a return message and click on the send button.

 **Try** *this*

- Send an email to a friend or teacher in another school

- Collect the reply and send a response.

Tip

When you send a reply the original message is still attached. You keep a copy of the original message, but if you keep using the reply button time after time you end up sending several messages each time. These take up more memory and therefore take longer to send. Only use **Reply** once or twice on the same message, then start a new message.

K Key *words*

Email address: the address
used to send a message to a
person's email account

Using the address book

It is a chore to type in **email addresses** and it is easy to make
mistakes. You can use your address book for ones you use frequently.

The easiest way to add a name to the address book is to look at a
message sent by that person.

Click the right mouse button on the sender's name. Click on **Add
Sender to Address Book** from the menu.

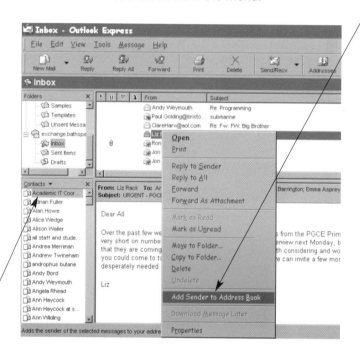

Next time you want to send a
message to that person, just
double click on their name in the
Contacts window.

Sending an attachment

You can also send files by email. A file can be sent as an **attachment**.
You will need to make sure that the recipient has suitable software
with which to open the file. Files sent as attachments should be as
small as possible to avoid expense to the sender or recipient.

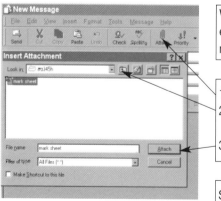

When using *Outlook Express*,
enter an address and type a
message as usual.

1. Click on the **Attach** button.
2. **Browse** to select the file to
   attach.
3. Click on the **Attach** button.

Send your message in the usual
way. It may take a few seconds
to send because the attachment
will take up more memory than
a plain email message.

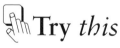**Try** *this*

■ Add an address to your
address book from a message
you have received.

■ Send a worksheet or planning
file to a colleague.

Changing the appearance of your messages

You can change the appearance of your emails by altering the background colour or font in the **New Message** window. A picture can used as the background for a message, but this often makes the text hard to read. You may want to use the school colours or a particular scheme.

Select **Background** from the **Format** menu. Choose a suitable colour.

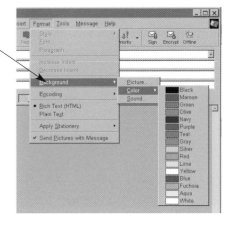

Change the style and size of the font using the tools on the text toolbar.

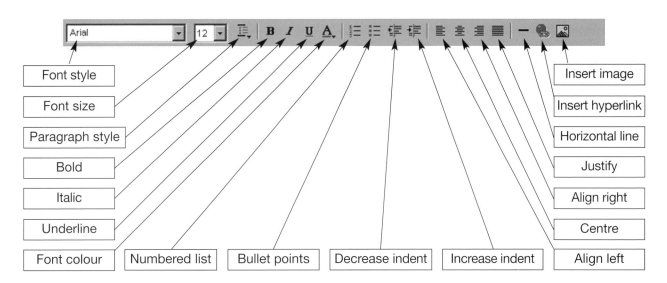

✋**Try** *this*

■ Send an email to a friend or colleague.

■ How is it different from writing a letter?

Change the style and size of the font using the tools on the text toolbar.

Font style	Insert image
Font size	Insert hyperlink
Paragraph style	Horizontal line
Bold	Justify
Italic	Align right
Underline	Centre
Font colour · Numbered list · Bullet points · Decrease indent · Increase indent	Align left

⚠ **Teaching** *idea:* *Geography/history*

Children can communicate with children in contrasting areas of the country. During a local study or study of a contrasting locality, they could exchange data about housing, employment, transport, industry, weather etc.

Video and sound

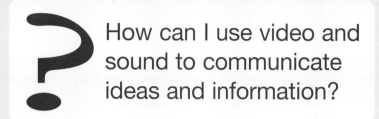

? How can I use video and sound to communicate ideas and information?

How it works

Presentation, multimedia authoring and web publishing software allows you to include video and sound in your work. This increases the range of media available to you and therefore the methods of communication. Care needs to be taken to ensure that these media are used to enhance the message rather than obscure it.

This type of software usually comes with a selection of video and sound files which can be used in the creation of materials. It is also possible to use files from the Internet, free CDs or to create your own. In order to include video and sound clips in your work, all you need are some basic file handling skills.

The techniques

Video

Video and animated graphics are available from the same sources as images and can be inserted into documents in much the same way.

All Microsoft software comes with a selection of animations and video clips. The contents will vary according to which versions of software you have. The **Clip Gallery** can be used to locate a suitable clip.

These animations can be used by teachers to present information in more motivating ways. Children need to be taught how to use them in an appropriate manner, according to the task in hand. The purpose, size and positioning of animations will need to be discussed.

Depending on the software, you may be able to insert a video directly onto the page. You may need to create a video frame or there may be one already placed on the page for you to use.

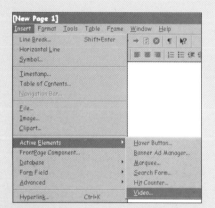

Front Page *allows you to insert a video or animation directly onto the page by selecting* **Active Elements** *from the* **Insert** *menu. Then click on* **Video** *and locate an appropriate file.*
To insert animated Clip Art, select **Clip Art** *from the* **Insert** *menu and click on the* **Motion Clips** *tab within the Clip Gallery.*

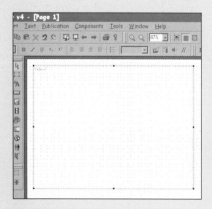

Illuminatus *requires you to create a video frame using the button on the vertical toolbar. A dialogue box will then appear asking you to choose a video file. There is no browser to view images, so you will need to know the file name and location in advance.*

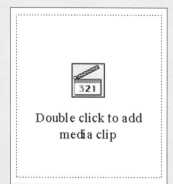

Double click to add media clip

PowerPoint *provides you with a video frame when you choose this type of slide layout. Double click in the video frame to activate the* **Clip Gallery** *and choose a motion clip.*
To insert a video clip from a different source, select **Movies and Sounds** *from the* **Insert** *menu and click on* **Movie** *from* **File**.

Inserting video clips

You are most likely to use video clips within multimedia publications, although they can also be put to effective use within presentations and web pages. It is best to collect appropriate clips, to fit in with the plan of the publication. These should be saved together in a folder ready for use.

1. Click on the **Video** button and draw a frame on the page.

2. Click on **Browse** in the **Video Properties** dialogue box and locate the clip you want to insert.

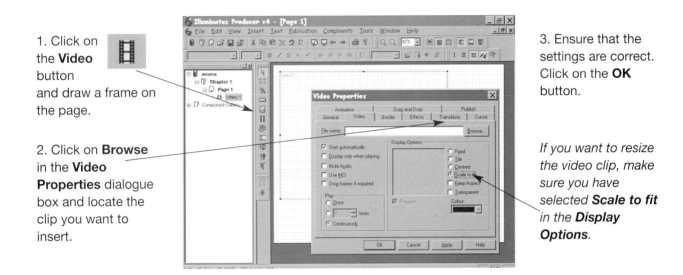

3. Ensure that the settings are correct. Click on the **OK** button.

If you want to resize the video clip, make sure you have selected Scale to fit in the Display Options.

Video properties

The properties of the video frame can be controlled. Children will need to be taught to consider the ways in which choices about presentation can affect the way the audience interacts with the information and ideas being communicated.

Illuminatus allows you to control the properties of any frame.

Frames can be **animated**, so that they bounce around the screen.

Frames can be a variety of shapes, not just rectangular.

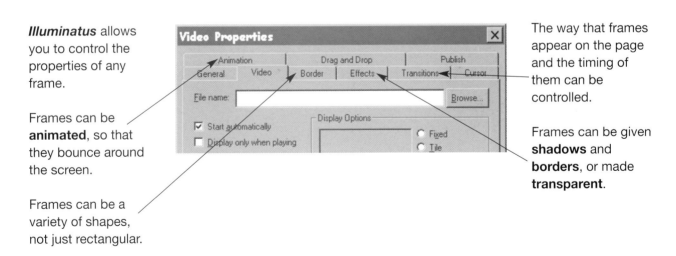

The way that frames appear on the page and the timing of them can be controlled.

Frames can be given **shadows** and **borders**, or made **transparent**.

Once you have placed a video clip on the page, it can be viewed using the **Preview** buttons. You will only see transitions, animations and videos in this mode.

Videos and animations from the Internet

You can search for and save videos and animations from the Internet in exactly the same way as still images. These can then be inserted into **video frames**.

You can use a **search engine** to search for video files.

By typing a subject in the search box, you can find videos on almost any subject. Click on a video to view the web site it comes from. You can then watch and save the clip you require.

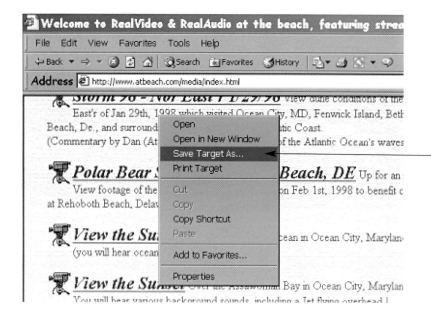

To save a video from a web site, put the pointer on the title and click the right hand mouse button. Click on **Save Target As** on the menu. Save the video into a folder to start a collection of videos on a theme or for a project.

Try *this*

- Use a search engine to find a selection of animations or video clips on a subject you will be teaching next term.

- Which of these offers more than a still image would in terms of information or motivation? Why?

Key *words*

Video frame: a frame drawn on the screen in which a video clip or animation can be placed

Motion Clips: video or animated clips

Video Properties dialogue box: a dialogue box which allows you to control the appearance and timing of a video or animated clip

Scale to fit: applied to images to avoid distortion and keep the proportions of the image the same regardless of size

Preview: run a presentation or multimedia resource as it will be seen by the audience

Adding sound effects

Sound effects and music can be added to presentations, multimedia packages and web sites. Sound files are usually associated with a particular page or event.

Sounds from the Internet

There are many types of sound files. The most common are **wav** and **midi files**. Recently **mp3 files** have also become available from the Internet. You can search for these on the Internet, using a **search engine**.

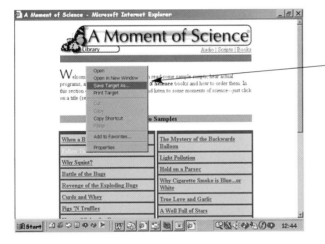

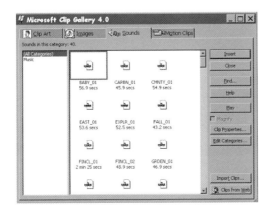

Sounds from the Clip Gallery

Sounds are also available from the Clip Gallery. As with images and video clips, it is advisable to collect and store sound files in one folder ready to use while you work. This is more efficient than searching for them as you go along.

By typing a subject in the search box, you can find sound clips on almost any subject. Click on a title to view the web site it comes from. You can then listen to and save the clip you require.

To save a sound file from a web site, put the pointer on the title and click the right hand mouse button. Click on **Save Target As** on the menu. Save the sound into a folder to start a collection of sound clips on a theme or for a project.

Associating a sound file with a page

A sound or music file can be associated with a page. The music will play when the page appears on the screen.

When using **Illuminatus**, double click on the page background to access the **Page Properties** dialogue box. Click on the **Sound** tab.

You can choose to play a track from a **CD**, but the CD must be present when the publication runs in order to hear the music, the file cannot be saved with the publication.

Click on **Play**, then **Browse** to locate the sound file you want to add.

Decide how long you want the music to play for and at what volume.

When you have selected the correct options, click on **OK**.

You will only hear the music when you run or preview the publication.

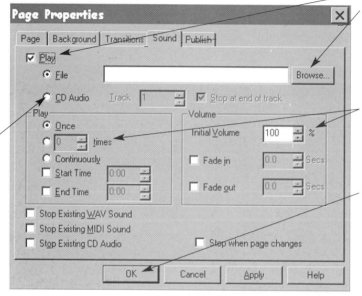

Associating a sound file with an event

You can use sound effects to draw attention to a particular point being made on screen. This is useful during presentations, but should be used sparingly to avoid distracting the audience from the content.

To associate a sound with the appearance of an image or text you must first add a visual effect or animation. The sound effect is then associated with that event.

When using **PowerPoint**, select **Custom Animation** from the **Slide Show** menu and select an animation.

Select a suitable sound effect.

Click on **Preview** to see and hear the effects. Click **OK** when you are satisfied with results.

Run the presentation to see and hear the sound effects in full screen mode.

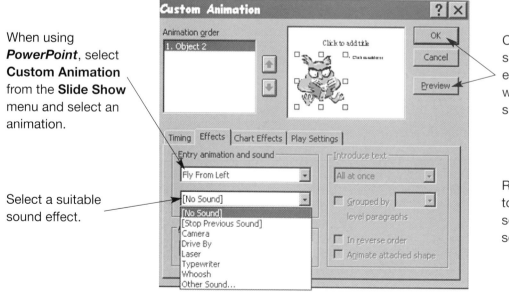

Projecting your work

Certain facilities are needed in order to model ICT techniques effectively. Teachers would not attempt to model handwriting without a large board on which do so or model reading without a text. It can be very difficult to teach a whole class effectively using a single monitor. There are several possible solutions to this:

● A large monitor can be used (at least 17 inch)
● A large TV can be plugged in to the computer
● A data projector can be used with a whiteboard or screen

The data projector is by far the most practical solution, but is also the most expensive. It will cost as much as 1 or 2 computers, but will be an invaluable tool for teaching and learning. When spending money on ICT equipment, buying as many computers as possible is not always the most effective strategy. The educational benefits of other hardware and software should also be considered.

A data projector can be portable. It can be used with desktop and laptop computers to demonstrate ICT skills and use ICT to teach other subjects.

An interactive whiteboard can be used with a data projector to allow the teacher to model techniques on the board. It also allows children to contribute to whole class activities and can save hand-written notes.

! Teaching *idea: Geography/ history/design technology*

Children can produce a multimedia guide to the school or local area to be shown to new parents and pupils. This could form part of a local study and include geographical and historical information. The design and production process would also develop D&T skills. They would need to examine currently available guides on paper and the Internet. Planning would form a large part of the project, images and text would need to be collected and/or created. Actual production could take place with groups of children being responsible for different sections of the guide. It would need to be evaluated and edited before 'going public'.

Try *this*

■ Create a presentation or multimedia publication to be used to introduce a new topic to the whole class.

■ Use video, animation and sound carefully to enhance points made.

■ How does this differ from using pictures or a TV programme?

■ What are the advantages to using multimedia software?

Presenting and sharing

How can I present and share information using multimedia?

How it works

Once the content and structure of a multimedia presentation or web site have been established and constructed, it is important to consider how the audience will experience the publication. In the case of a presentation, it may be that you have the opportunity to introduce the material. However, a multimedia publication or web site must also be usable without any introduction, or must contain some explanation of how it should be used.

There are issues of appearance which need to be considered, such as the movement and style of transitions between pages and events and the navigation strategy. You must also decide how and why the audience will use your publication, e.g. on screen, on paper, with help etc.

Good quality web sites have clear links to other pages and sites. Graphics are used sparingly and appropriately. Summary information is provided to help you to choose which sections are most useful.

In general, there is little point in printing multimedia resources, as the multimedia features are lost. It can be useful to print a summary for your audience. If the publication is to be presented on screen, there are issues of the method, e.g. saving to CD or uploading to the Internet.

It is also possible to send files via email. These can include multimedia files, although there are issues of size and memory. Sharing information using email is fast, cheap and versatile.

[K] Key *words*

Uploading: publishing a web site on the Internet

Transitions: the visual effect used to move from one page to another

Navigation: the method by which you view and move around information

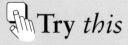 Try *this*

Look at a web site or CD-ROM. Explore how easy it is to use. Examine the navigation tools and special effects. They should enhance the content rather than detract from it.

The techniques

Transitions

You can control the way in which elements and slides appear on the screen using **transitions**. This can add to the professional appearance of your presentation or web site.

The way that each page or slide appears on the screen can be varied according to purpose and audience. You can also control the transition of individual elements on the page or slide. This allows the presenter to order the appearance of frames on the screen.

Try *this*

- Add a spectacular transition to a title slide to make an impression and grab the audience's attention.

- Add transition effects to the pages. You may wish them all to follow the same pattern or choose different effects to suit the contents of the pages.

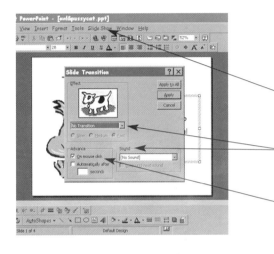

When using Microsoft *Power Point*, select **Slide Transition** from the **Slide Show menu**. Select a transition and sound effect. You can also choose whether to trigger the transition with a mouse click or after a set amount of time.

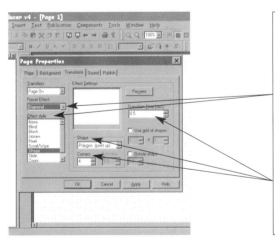

When using *Illuminatus*, double click on the page background to access the **Page Properties** dialogue box. Click on the **Transition** tab. Select a transition effect. You can also control the features of the transition using the **Shape**, **Corners** and **Timing** options. Preview the transition before clicking on **OK**.

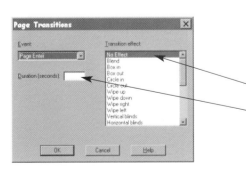

When using Microsoft *Front Page*, select **Page transition** from the **Format menu**. Choose a transition from the list provided and choose the amount of time it takes.

Linking pages and events

Buttons and links can be used to trigger events and actions on the screen. These can be linked to other events on a page, other sections of a document, other documents or web sites.

Traditional buttons can be created, but pictures and text can also be **hot spots** or **hyperlinks**. It is important that buttons and links are made clear and that they follow a logical pattern throughout the presentation or web site.

A multimedia publication contains buttons and hyperlinks to move the user to other pages. These can be images, words or symbols.

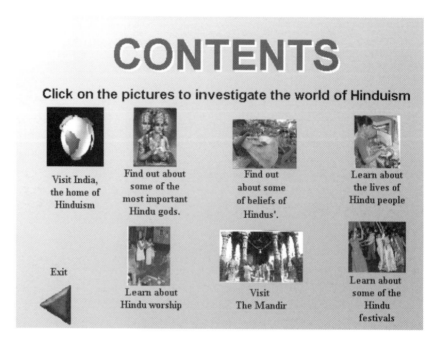

Buttons

Buttons are the simplest way of linking pages together. This is particularly important when you are creating a multimedia publication or web site for others to use. The links between pages should be carefully planned when you are considering the structure of your work. Remember to include a 'back' or 'home' button on most pages.

Multimedia authoring software, such as *Illuminatus*, usually includes a button tool. Click on it and draw a button on the page. The size and position of the button can be altered at any time.

When you have drawn a button, the **Button Actions** dialogue box will automatically appear.

🄚 Key *words*

Hyperlink: a link between different marked places in a document or between documents

Hot spots: a link between different marked places in a document or between documents

Button actions

The **Trigger** tab allows you to choose what action triggers the button. This is usually best left as the left mouse click.

The **Goto/Show** tab enables you to use the button to move to another page, show or hide an object on the page, close the window or exit from the publication.

The **Play** tab can be used to make the button start a video, sound file or CD track.

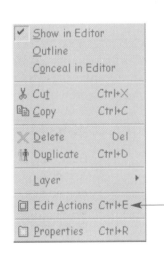

To return to the Button Actions dialogue box at any time, right click the mouse on the button on your page and select **Edit Action.**

To change the appearance of the button, double click on it. Click on the **Button** tab. You can alter the colour, bevel or even put a picture on it.

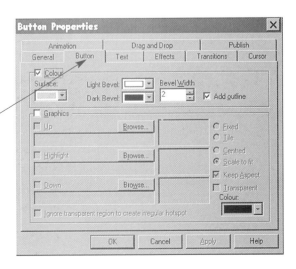

K Key *words*

Hyperlink: a link between different marked places in a document or between documents

Hot spots: a link between different marked places in a document or between documents

URL: Uniform Resource Locator or web address

! Teaching *idea: English*

Children could create a simple web page containing information about a recent school trip. They may use a template created by the teacher. Hyperlinks could be added to link to the web site of the attraction visited and other related sites. This page could be added to the school web site for use by parents, pupils, governors and other schools. The children should consider their audience when designing and creating the page. The writing itself should be of a discursive nature, presenting opinions and editorial about the location visited.

Try *this*

Create a web page to support teaching and learning for a curriculum topic for your class or year group. Find some useful web sites for teachers and pupils to use for planning and research. Make a list of the sites and create a hyperlink to each one.

Pictures as links

A picture can be used as a button. Insert a picture onto your page and click the right mouse button on it. Select **Edit Actions** from the menu that appears. Use the same techniques as with the button.

You will need to add a text box near the image on the page so that the user knows that the image will trigger another event.

Hyperlinks

A hyperlink can link to a web site, perhaps to give further information on a particular subject. Text or an image can be used as a hyperlink. When creating a web site, it is often useful to use hyperlinks to other pages within your site and direct users to other related sites.

Front Page allows you to add hyperlinks to your web pages simply and quickly. When the page is previewed or viewed in a browser, hyperlinked text will appear underlined and a hyperlinked image will have a blue border around it.

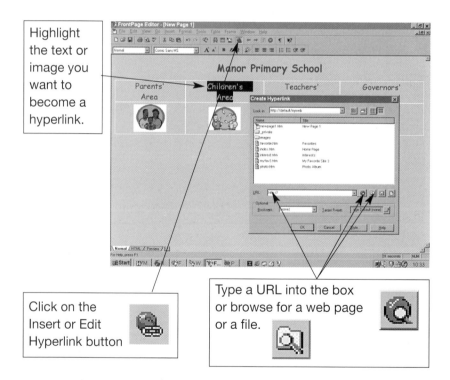

Highlight the text or image you want to become a hyperlink.

Click on the Insert or Edit Hyperlink button

Type a URL into the box or browse for a web page or a file.

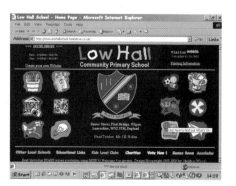

Designing a school web site

When designing school web pages, it is important that the audience is identified. Many of the users may be children, so the use of images as well as text can make it easier for them to navigate around the site. Alternative text appears when the pointer is placed on a hyperlink. This can help children and adults to understand the use of images.

Publishing to disk

Multimedia presentations can be created and viewed on computers on which the correct software is installed. There may be occasions on which you wish to demonstrate this type of resource in a different locality where you are not sure of the software available. It is possible to save the presentation in such a way that it will run on any computer, this is called **publishing** it. This takes up slightly more memory than saving the work normally.

When using **Illuminatus**, make sure your work is saved. Select **Publish** from the **Publication** menu.

Select a location to publish to, perhaps onto a floppy disk or other portable media.

Follow the instructions and test the publication.

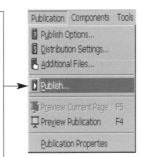

Try *this*

- Publish a multimedia publication to a floppy disk or zip disk and run it on a machine without the software installed on it.

- Contact your Internet Service Provider to get a web address and password.

- Upload a simple web site you and/or the children have created.

Once your work has been published to disk, the published version cannot be edited. You will need to repeat this process in order to make any changes to the presentation.

Uploading a web site

Once a web site has been created, it needs to be **uploaded** to the Internet so that it can be viewed by a world wide audience. You will need to obtain a web address and password from your Internet Service Provider; this can be done by telephone.

Make sure the web site is saved on your computer first.

Click on the **Publish Web** button on the toolbar.

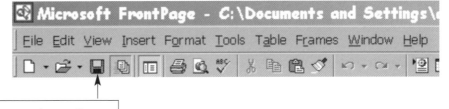

Type in the URL for your web site, given to you by your Internet Service Provider.

Provide the password given to you by your ISP.

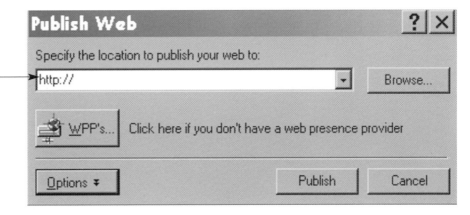

When you update your web site, just save and repeat this process to update the information accessible on the Internet. Your web site should be updated regularly to avoid an unprofessional appearance and to make efficient use of the media.

Printing

Once a multimedia publication has been created, whether it is a presentation or web site, it is best viewed on screen. This enables the audience or user to view the full range of effects and features.

There are times when it is useful to be able to print all or part of multimedia work.
- It can be useful during the planning process, to see the whole publication and review the structure and overall appearance.
- If the work contains a lot of text, it can be easier to read on paper, whilst editing on screen.
- When giving a presentation, notes pages providing thumbnails of slides can provide the audience with an *aide memoire* and opportunity to see the overall pattern and form of the information.
- For assessment and marking purposes it can be useful to see a selection of pages printed out.

Try *this*

■ Print out a navigation plan of a web site you or the children have created.

■ Print out thumbnails of slides to accompany a presentation for a staff meeting.

When using **Front Page**, you can print the structure of the web site. In **Front Page Explorer** select the **Navigation** view.

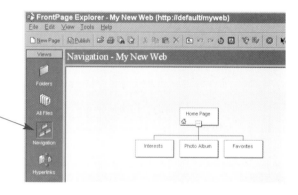

K Key *words*

Thumbnail: a miniature version of an image

Navigation view: screen which shows the way in which pages are linked together

Select **Print Navigation View** from the **File menu**.

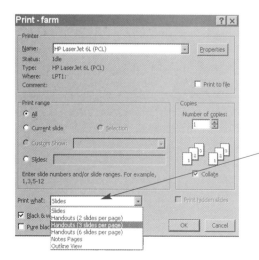

When using **PowerPoint**, select **Print** from the **File** menu. You can then choose what to print.
- 1 slide to a page
- 2 slides to a page
- 3 slides to a page with lines for the audience to make notes
- 6 slides to a page
- Notes pages for the presenter and/or audience
- Outline view for a summary of the text

Printing handouts

When using **PowerPoint** it is possible to print out handouts to accompany a presentation. While using the presentation, the audience can refer to the notes and use them to write notes. Presentation software is designed to be used to communicate ideas to a large audience using visual and sound effects to highlight key points. The slides should contain the main points of the information, but not too much text. Graphics and special effects should be used with care to present ideas clearly rather than confuse the audience.

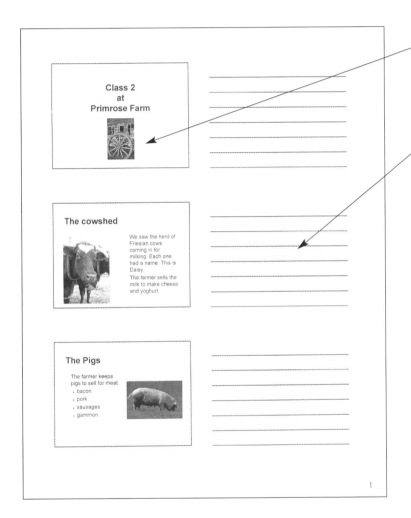

Slides and images can be printed out in black and white, saving expensive printing ink.

Space for notes to be made beside each slide enables children to make editing comments or adults to add extra information for their own use.

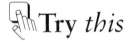

! Teaching *idea:* *Design and technology*

Children review the structure of a web site they have created. Print the Navigation View and use as a focus for discussion of the organisation of the pages. Discuss the hierarchy and grouping of pages and possible alternatives.

Try *this*

- Open a presentation containing pictures to be used to introduce a new topic in the classroom.

- Print 3 slides to a page.

- Give out to pairs of children to be used for note taking and brainstorming during a class discussion.

Teaching and learning with ICT

Section content

This section of the book is divided into two parts.
- Lesson planning: general ideas for how to plan, manage and assess ICT work
- Classroom activities: sample lessons with guidance notes.

When using ICT with children, you need to take a range of planning issues into account. Many of these are the same as for work without ICT. Others however, are ones that may be new and for which new solutions are needed. Planning the use of ICT involves:
- lesson planning
- management
- assessment.

Most of these issues will be the similar no matter what kinds of ICT activities are being carried out. It is also the case that because of the differences in hardware, software and ICT systems in each school, there can be no single definitive solution to the various problems and issues that occur. Issues and problems need to be identified and solutions found to either minimise or overcome them.

Lesson planning

These notes refer to how a lesson using ICT can be planned before the lesson to ensure that teaching and learning aims and objectives can be achieved.
- *Aims and outcomes:* relate the lesson aims and outcomes to both the subject Orders and to the Orders for ICT.
- *ICT resources:* use of computers will be determined by the hardware and software that is available but it is important to work towards ensuring that this factor is minimised.
- *Access to ICT:* consider whether ICT must be used by all children during one lesson or whether it is possible to stage their access over a longer period.
- *Choice of applications:* work towards ensuring that children have a choice of ICT applications and software so that their use of ICT can become progressively independent.
- *Knowledge and techniques:* check whether children can use the ICT techniques needed for the lesson, or ensure that your lesson plan includes time to teach them.

- *Differentiation:* devise ways to achieve differentiation by using ICT and other methods, for example by writing alternative versions of documents and giving access to different resources.
- *Backup:* make sure you have a backup plan in case any part of the ICT system cannot be made to work effectively.

Lesson management

These notes consider how the lesson can be managed while it is being taught. The main concerns here are with technical matters relating to ensuring the effective use of hardware and software.

- *Number of computers:* the teacher's time and focus will be affected by whether all children are working with ICT at the same time in an ICT suite or if only small numbers are working on one or more stand-alone computers.
- *Running programs:* programs need to be installed and made accessible, for example on a computer's hard drive, on a network or from a floppy disc or CD-Rom.
- *Assistance:* access to technical assistance can be invaluable during a lesson that involves ICT because without it, even relatively simple technical problems can cause the ICT work to be abandoned.
- *ICT capacity:* ensure that the ICT system has the capacity to run the programs you need to use, for example that CD-Roms can be run across a network or that files you produce at home have compatible formats to what is available in school.
- *On-screen or hard copy:* consider whether the work can be done on-screen or if desk space is needed for hard copy resources.
- *Demonstration:* consider how you will be able to demonstrate ICT techniques, for example by a projector or if this needs to be done in other ways.
- *Seating:* check on how children will be seated so that you can position yourself appropriately when monitoring and to see if individual or group work can be done.
- *Health and safety:* check for any potential hazards such as leads and sockets.
- *Lighting:* check that lighting in the room is suitable for working on a monitor and that you will be able to demonstrate on a screen that will be visible.

- *Heating:* make sure that there is adequate ventilation, even when there are security implications for the room.
- *Printing:* consider if the children's work needs to be printed and how this could be done bearing in mind cost and the time printing can take into account.

Assessment of children's ICT work

Assessment raises a range of issues that relate to subject criteria for assessment, identifying children's work and in how to access it.

- *Marking criteria:* consider how the marking criteria for ICT work compares with work produced without a computer, for example with regard to neatness or to specific subject criteria.
- *Access to work:* consider the options to access children's work, for example as printouts, on disc or by email.
- *Fairness:* consider how you will handle the fact that some children will have access to hardware and software at home while others will not.
- *Marking:* make use of ICT to improve your own marking, recording and feedback of children's work.
- *Identifying work:* use monitoring and other methods to ensure that you can identify the work done by different children, especially when work is done as a group but also when it ought to be done individually.
- *ICT and subject:* you may need to devise a marking system that records achievement in both subject work and ICT work.

Key points

Some of these problems and issues can be resolved by a variety of technological solutions. Others require nothing more than adapting standard classroom practices. The following items are key points to success:

- lesson planning that includes clear reasoning as to why ICT is being used
- long-term planning to ensure regular access to ICT for all children
- co-ordinated planning to ensure that children are taught ICT techniques that are needed for subject work
- checking ICT equipment to ensure that it works in the way you need to use it
- knowledge of the hardware and software so that basic problems can be quickly resolved
- a willingness to experiment and to share experiences with others
- a determination to develop ICT hardware, software and systems so that it meets your teaching and learning needs, rather than allowing it to determine and limit what you want to do.

Most teachers find that early use of ICT can be difficult but that with lesson evaluations that identify the nature of the problems and with persistence, their ICT work becomes easier and more enjoyable both for themselves and for the children.

Into the classroom

Subject work

This section presents sample activities for use with children on how to use ICT to present and share information and ideas using multimedia. The activities are intended to be illustrative of what can be done, rather than attempting to provide ready-made resources.

Four subjects have been chosen to illustrate these ideas:
- English
- Design and Technology
- History
- Geography

All the activities can also contribute to work for the NC orders for ICT. There will also be links to the National Literacy and Numeracy Strategies.

The activities

All the tools and techniques needed to create and work with the sample activities have been described in the previous sections. In most cases the ICT techniques that children need to produce multimedia publications are limited to the presentation of text, images and sound. They will, of course, require a different range of skills to gather these resources.

The activities are deliberately ICT-rich. Teachers may need to adapt some elements to suit the capabilities of pupils and staff involved. The level and organisation of ICT resources in the school may also affect the way in which the activities are used.

ICT: planning, management, teaching and assessment

ICT can be used to greatly enhance and extend teaching and learning opportunities. When planning to use ICT with primary pupils, the key questions to ask are:

- Does ICT provide unique opportunities for teaching and learning?

  or

- Does ICT allow the teacher and/or pupils to achieve the learning objective more effectively or efficiently?

If the answer to both of these questions is "No", then it is probably not the most suitable vehicle for teaching and learning in the lesson.

It is difficult to give definitive guidance on the planning, management, teaching and assessment of work with ICT. This is because so much depends on the ICT resources in each school and the way that schemes of work are written. Working with one computer in a classroom requires a very different approach to using computers in an ICT suite. Some activities are more suited to one model than the other, but many can be used in either with some consideration of classroom management and organisation. Access to computer facilities for all children must be carefully written into schemes of work and lesson plans, irrespective of how teaching is organised.

Some suggestions on how children could use each activity in the classroom are provided. Key points are raised as relevant to the activities, though many of the issues are likely to be generic. Access to a computer and a printer for example, applies to almost all ICT work.

Lessons that make use of ICT may have dual learning objectives, for ICT and another subject. This has implications for assessment, however this is not a new challenge. Teachers often assess children's use of English or Mathematics during other subject lessons. With careful planning and monitoring, lesson time can be made more productive in a busy timetable.

Sample activity   KS1 English

Farm Trip Diary

Aim

To recount events of a class trip, including headings, sub-headings, picture captions and labels for diagrams.

Setting the scene

We visited a farm. We learned about the different kinds of animals which live there and how the farmer looks after them. A diary of the day should report the events accurately and be entertaining for the audience. The information must be well organised, using appropriate language and pictures.

Activity

In this activity you will create a multimedia diary of a day trip to the farm. Use the slides containing the pictures taken with the digital camera. Add headings and text to each slide to create an entertaining slide show to show to the rest of the school during a class assembly. You will use **PowerPoint** to present your information.

1. Watch the slide show of the photographs taken during the visit.

- What is happening in each photograph?
- Are the photographs in the right order?
- What information needs to be written on each slide?
- What style of writing should be used?

2. Add a title and caption to each slide.

- Type your ideas onto the slide.
- Use the shift key to use capital letters in the correct places.
- Use the delete key to remove words and phrases.
- Type in new words and phrases.
- Read your work and make sure you have written full sentences.
- Save your work.

3. Watch the whole slide show with the class.

- Are the headings suitable?
- Is there anything missing from the captions?
- Is the punctuation correct?
- Which font would be suitable to use for clear presentation to the whole school during an assembly?
- What are the features of this font that make it suitable?
- What special effects would improve the presentation?
- What should be included on a title slide?

Make any changes needed to your slides.

- What are the benefits of using ICT?
- What could be done that would be impossible using other media?
- How has ICT helped to present the diary in an appropriate way for an assembly?

Sample work

Children can work in groups to produce presentations. This provides many opportunities to develop their collaborative skills and share ideas. They can all contribute to the work, without having to worry about their handwriting or presentation skills.

ICT Techniques

- Choosing a layout
- Entering and formatting text
- Bullet points and lists
- Images from other sources
- Inserting images
- Associating a sound file with an event
- Presenting to an audience

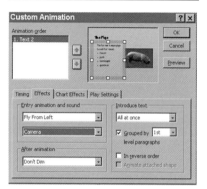

*Visual and sound effects can be added by selecting **Custom Animation** from the **Slide Show** menu.*

Sample work

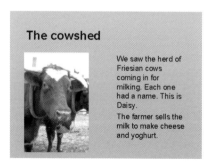

Ask the children to recount the events of the day and what they learned about the farm and animals.

Children's work   English activity

1. Whole class work and teacher demonstration
   The whole class watches a slide show of photographs taken during the trip. This has been prepared in advance by the teacher using photographs taken with a digital camera or scanned in. Ideally a data projector, a large monitor or TV will be used. Demonstrate how to move from one slide to the next using a single mouse click. Explain that the finished slide show will be used during a class assembly and shown to the whole school.

   Each slide will also contain a text frame for the title and one for an accompanying caption. Discuss the audience and purpose of the presentation and what style the writing should take, e.g. chronological, accurate, direct, impersonal etc. Demonstrate how to add text to the frames, how to edit, delete and insert text.

2. Independent work
   Divide up the slides so that the children, working in pairs or small groups, have one or two headings and captions to write depending on ability. Children open the appropriate file, with adult help if necessary, and work directly onto the screen, typing titles and text.

   Children may need some encouragement to discuss and edit the content, grammar and punctuation of the text as they work.

   Some children will be able to write more and provide more detail about the animals and farming as well as recounting events. They can add a simple structure to their writing using bullet points. Children should save the work regularly, with adult help if necessary.

3. Whole class work and teacher demonstration
   View the whole slide show with the class. (The slides may need to be collated if children have been working on separate computers.) Discuss the language used and the suitability of headings. Edit text if necessary, asking the authors to make changes on screen.

   Review the different fonts and sizes available, discuss what type of font is needed and choose one which is appropriate for the whole school audience. This can be demonstrated by the teacher and carried out by children on their own slides.

Explore and discuss the visual and sound special effects available and add to the slide show to enhance the diary. This can be demonstrated by the teacher.

View the whole presentation, discussing the effects of the changes made.

Discuss the possibility of printing the presentation. The visual and sound effects will be lost, but the content will remain well organised and structured. If printed the presentation will become a class book, with a smaller audience when read.

Children's work

NC English KS1

En1 Speaking and listening
3d extend their ideas in the light of discussion
8c describing events and experiences
8d speaking to different people, including friends, the class, teachers and other adults
10b sharing ideas and experiences

En3 Writing
1b sequence events and recount them in appropriate detail
1e vary their writing to suit the purpose and reader
2b assemble and develop ideas on paper and on screen
2c plan and review their writing, discussing the quality of what is written
5h the importance of clear and neat presentation in order to communicate meaning effectively
11 The range of readers for writing should include teachers, other adults, children and the writers themselves.

Planning

These activities form part of KS1 work in English on writing non-fiction texts. The on-screen work will also help to develop the children's ICT skills.

The activities use text entry and formatting tools in a presentation package. The teacher will need to prepare a series of slides in advance, each containing an image, a text frame for the title and a text frame for the caption. The children need to know how to enter text into frames, use the delete and shift keys and the space bar.

During the whole class sections of the activity children will have opportunities to learn how to change the style and size of the font and add visual and sound effects to the presentation.

Management

Some method of projection is ideally needed for this activity, however a large monitor or TV screen could be used instead. The final presentation would also have to be scaled down if a data projector is not available.

Teaching and learning

This is an activity best carried out with the children working in pairs or small groups. Some may benefit from adult support. Discussion and collaboration should be encouraged throughout. The class is effectively creating a class book and all should feel involved.

Teaching

The content of the slide show is first presented and explained by the teacher. Discussion of the layout and content should encourage children to share their ideas. The emphasis of the activity is on the quality of the content rather than the appearance of the text.

The children can be involved in choosing and changing the style and size of the font and adding special effects to the slide show. It should be stressed that these choices are not just a matter of subjective taste, but should be related to the audience and purpose of the writing.

Assessment

This activity provides opportunities for assessment in English and ICT, in particular non-fiction writing, collaboration, word processing, speaking and listening skills. Some children may also be involved in some small-scale research to add information to their slide.

Formative assessment will take place throughout the activity, particularly through intervention during independent work and discussion during whole class sections. The final presentation will provide evidence of the knowledge and skills which have been developed during the activity. The work can be printed out in book form to be used by different audiences.

The problem with on screen work is in knowing how the work was done and sometimes, who did it. The teacher or other adults involved will need to monitor closely how the work is completed if the work of each child is to be assessed separately. Some self assessment and record keeping can help in this respect.

Techniques used by teacher

- Choosing slide layouts
- Adding a background
- Adding visual special effects
- Adding sound effects

Techniques used by children

- Entering text
- Formatting text
- Using bullet points

Sample activity   KS2 Design and Technology

Multimedia Adventure Game

Aim

To plan, produce and evaluate a structured, multimedia adventure game for use by younger children.

Setting the scene

There are many adventure games available for KS1 children. They develop skills of prediction and logic and encourage young children to work together to solve problems. They should be visually stimulating, with short, simple text and should be fun to play.

Activity

You are going to design and make your own computer adventure game. You will use text, pictures and sounds to create a series of linked pages. It will be designed for and evaluated by KS1 children in your school.

1. Do you remember what adventure games you liked to play in your KS1 classes? Collect two or three games from the current KS1 classes and play them.
   - What is the game about?
   - How is it structured?
   - Do the KS1 children enjoy playing it?
   - What do they like or dislike about it?
   - How could it be improved?
   - Is it easy to read the instructions and story?
   - What decisions have to be made?

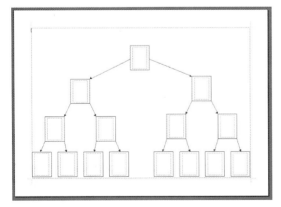

2. Use the information you have gathered to design your own game.
   - Start with a traditional story
   - Make a flow chart showing the different options and pathways through the story
   - Children should be able to choose what happens in the story, each page will give them a choice or a decision to make
   - Make sure you show which pages are connected
   - List what will be on each page, including text, pictures, sounds and buttons.

3. Collect the resources you will need. You may need to gather pictures and sounds from the Internet or a CD. It is best to save them all in one folder on the hard disk or on a floppy disk. Make sure that each file is named sensibly so that you know which ones to use on each page of your game.

4. Create and link the pages of the game. Stick to your plan and use the pictures and sounds you have collected to create the game. Make sure all the links are correct and working.

5. Ask a KS1 class to use and evaluate your game. Review your game and make any changes relating to the children's comments.

Children's work

Design & Technology activity

1. Discuss adventure games used at home and at school with the class. Pupils need to be able to identify the features of the games which make it appealing to them. In effect they are evaluating the software. They also need to consider the educational value of such games and why they are an important part of school ICT. Questions could be prepared or the children could identify what needs to be examined. The questions and answers could be typed straight into a word processor and used to develop a questionnaire.

   These ideas and questions then need to be applied to the development of a questionnaire for KS1 children. Older pupils may need to be reminded of the adventure games available in KS1. The results of the questionnaire should be used to produce a design for a new adventure game.

2. Set the pupils the task of starting with a traditional story and altering it so it has several different narratives and endings. They will work in small groups and choose a story from a limited selection. It may be helpful to read several versions of the same story.

   They will need to produce a flow chart of the game. This can be done on the computer or by hand. It should contain:
   - a summary of the story
   - notes about the pictures and sounds needed on each slide
   - arrows showing which pages are linked
   - ideas about backgrounds, buttons, transitions, colour schemes, fonts etc.

   The teacher could prepare a template in advance so that the plans all follow the same pattern. Using text boxes allows the quick production of a clear flow chart, which is flexible and easy to use.

Sample work

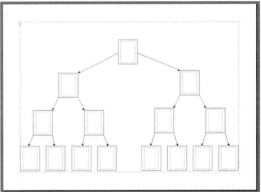

A flow chart can be produced using the text box and arrow drawing facilities in a word processor. Children can then type directly into the boxes or write on a printed sheet.

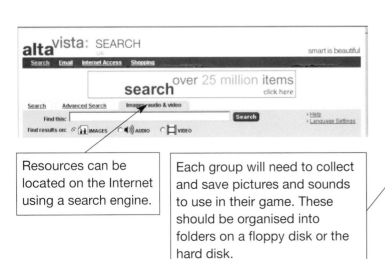

Resources can be located on the Internet using a search engine.

Each group will need to collect and save pictures and sounds to use in their game. These should be organised into folders on a floppy disk or the hard disk.

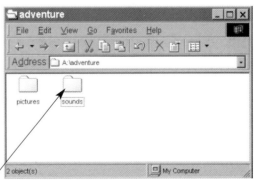

Sample work

Using a graduated background is a simple way of achieving a professional appearance.

Sample work

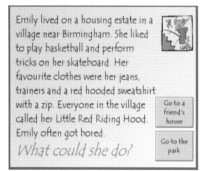

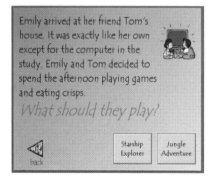

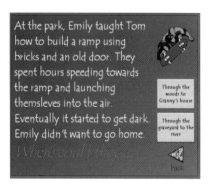

Buttons and navigation tools should be the same on each page. Keep them simple and easy to follow.

3. A list of resources can be made from the flow chart. Pictures and sounds are the most important elements. These can be gathered from the Internet or from CD-ROMs. They should be saved onto floppy disk or onto the hard disk. A filing structure will be needed for each group. It may be necessary to prepare this in advance.

4. Once the resources have been collected, the production of the adventure game can begin. Children should be encouraged to stick to their plan, considering the audience and purpose of the finished product when making decisions about appearance and content.

   Initial work should involve the layout and appearance of the pages. Backgrounds and fonts will be chosen to suit the contents of the slides and the overall feel of the game. Backgrounds should be used to convey atmosphere and the events on the pages, e.g. representing day and night.

   Fonts should be chosen carefully to suit the users of them game and to ensure clear communication of instructions and events, as well as adding to the overall appearance of the pages.

   Links between pages should be clear and easy to follow. The use of buttons or icons will make use of visual cues and will be easier for young children to follow. These should follow a consistent pattern throughout the game.

   Animations and sound effects can be added at this stage. They should be used to enhance the game, rather than detract from the content. Children should be encouraged to keep them brief and appropriate to the story. Simple animations such as the transitions between pages and page elements can also be added and should be used thoughtfully, perhaps following a pattern throughout.

   Once the game has been completed and saved, it should be thoroughly tested to make sure that all the buttons and links work properly.

5. The game can now be used by a KS1 class. They should be asked to evaluate it by answering the original list of questions:
   - What is the game about?
   - How is it structured?
   - Do you enjoy playing it?
   - What do you like or dislike about it?
   - Is it easy to read the instructions and story?
   - What decisions have to be made?
   - How could it be improved?

   This could be carried out as a data handling activity. The results should be used to make any final alterations to the game before saving it to disk.

   Many multimedia authoring and presentation packages have the facility to 'publish' work. This means that once saved, work can be run on machines which do not have the software installed on them. This would enable children to take work home and share it with other classes without the expense of having to buy several licences for the software.

Children's work

NC Design & Technology KS2

1a generate ideas for products after thinking about who will use them and what they will be used for, using information from a number of different sources, including ICT-based sources

1b develop ideas and explain them clearly, putting together a list of what they want their design to achieve

1c plan what they have to do, suggesting a sequence of actions and alternatives, if needed

1d communicate design ideas in different ways as these develop, bearing in mind aesthetic qualities, and the uses and purposes for which the product is intended

2e use finishing techniques to strengthen and improve the appearance of their product, using a range of equipment including ICT

3a reflect on the progress of their work as they design and make, identifying ways they could improve their products

3b carry out appropriate tests before making any improvements

3c recognise that the quality of a product depends on how well it is made and how well it meets its intended purpose

5a investigating and evaluating a range of familiar products, thinking about how they work, how they are used and the views of the people who use them

5b focused practical tasks that develop a range of techniques, skills, processes and knowledge

Planning

These activities form part of KS2 work in Design and Technology on designing, making and evaluating products. They also cover KS2 work in English on writing fiction for different audiences. The on-screen work will also help to develop the children's ICT skills. Word processing and multimedia authoring skills will be developed during this activity.

The activities use text and image entry and formatting techniques within a multimedia authoring package. Children will need to be taught how to collect and save resources before using them in the publication. Special effects can be added to the work with the teaching of a few further techniques. The use of sound and video files requires the application of skills developed through working with images.

Differentiated activities can be provided through the preparation of a basic structure for some children or

Teaching and learning

additional support where appropriate. It is likely that children's language capability may affect their engagement with these activities. Differentiation can also be achieved through the expectations of the outcome; some groups' work may have a simpler structure or use less text.

Management

Children need access to multimedia authoring software such as **Illuminatus** or **Hyper Studio**, although a similar result could be produced using presentation software such as **PowerPoint** or using the web design features of a word processor or DTP package. Some method of projection may be useful during whole class teaching and demonstration sessions.

KS2 pupils should be capable of typing ideas directly on screen and editing them as work progresses. The transferable skills should be emphasised to pupils so that they can make good use of their word processing and image manipulation skills in a new environment. This activity is best carried out with children working in pairs or small groups. Some may benefit from adult support. Discussion and collaboration should be encouraged throughout.

Teaching

The teacher introduces the concept of adventure games. The educational features should be discussed, along with the need for a clear structure and a content carefully designed for the target audience. Emphasis should be placed on detailed planning and coherent structure rather than busy pages and special effects. The multimedia features of the software should be used to enhance the content and motivate the target users.

The children can design their games on screen or on paper, but they will need to be familiar with the capabilities of the software to allow them to include them in their plans. This can be achieved through a demonstration of one of the sample files available or a more pertinent example created by the teacher.

The evaluation of products by the target audience forms an important part of the process. KS1 children may be involved at various stages of the project. Pupils should be encouraged to take their opinions into consideration when developing their work.

Children's work

Assessment

This activity provides opportunities for assessment in Design and Technology, English and ICT. In particular designing, making, evaluating, fiction writing for a given audience, collaboration and multimedia authoring skills can be monitored and assessed. Children may also be involved in research to identify what is needed in the games and to collect resources to be used in the work.

Techniques used by teacher

- Finding and providing resources

Teaching and learning

Formative assessment will take place throughout the activity, particularly through intervention during independent work and discussion during whole class sections. The final product will provide evidence of the knowledge and skills which have been developed during the activity. The work can be printed out in book form to be used, perhaps by a different audience from the multimedia game.

Techniques used by children

- Deciding on the content
- Creating a structure
- Entering and formatting text, images, videos and sounds
- Controlling the transitions between events
- Linking pages and events

Sample activity

Web guide to the local area

Aim

To carry out an historical investigation into the local area and present information using a web site for a wide and varied audience.

Setting the scene

Many people including tourists, local historians, teachers and pupils use a guide to the local history of an area. It needs to contain information from many sources covering a range of issues. Presenting this information in a web site allows people from all over the world to find out about a place. It must be written in a style suitable for such a wide and varied audience and contain accurate and up-to-date information.

Activity

Find and read some local history guide books, leaflets and web sites. These will be available from your local tourist office, library or museum.

1. Review and evaluate the content and layout of paper or web-based local guides. The content is the most important aspect:
   ● What is included?
   ● Is it easy to understand?
   ● Who is the leaflet/web site aimed at?
   ● Is the information interesting and accurate?
   ● How could it be improved?

   The appearance and layout are also important:
   ● How much space is taken up by text?
   ● How are pictures used?
   ● What fonts and colours are used?
   ● Is it eye-catching?
   ● Is it easy to read and find what you want?

   As a class, decide what needs to be included in a guide and share out the different areas to be covered.

2. The information you collect will form one page of a class web site about the local history of your town or area.

   You should create a plan or make sketches on paper before you start to create your web page. Any files you produce, pictures, charts, graphs, word processing etc. should be saved in one place so that you can insert them easily onto your page.
   ● How will you organise the page?
   ● What is the clearest layout to use?
   ● What font/s will you use?
   ● Will your page follow a template used by the whole class?
   ● Which colour scheme is best suited to the content and audience of your page?
   ● How will you use titles and sub-titles?
   ● How will you use pictures and graphics?

   As your guide is web-based, you could include hyperlinks to useful web sites you have found during your research. This might help you to cut down the amount of text you need on your page. You may want to consider including some short sound or video files to take advantage of the multimedia capability of ICT and present information in a stimulating way.

3. Research the area you have been given. You may need to collect information in a variety of forms:
   ● Primary evidence from interviews and photographs
   ● Data from census materials, records and maps
   ● Secondary evidence from newspaper reports and books.

   There are lots of places you can look to find this information. The local library or tourist office is a good place to start. Museums and churches will also provide useful information. You can also search on the Internet and use CD-ROMs. To find out about more recent historical events and developments you could interview local people and take photographs or scan images to illustrate the incidents and changes they describe.

4. Create a page using the background and colours you have chosen in your plan.

   Add the information and pictures you have collected to your page layout. Make sure your page is clear, interesting and suitable for the people who are going to be reading it. When it is finished, demonstrate and explain it to the class. You may wish to make some minor changes in the light of their comments.

Children's work   ## History activity

1. Examine and discuss a range of local history guides with the class. This should include paper and web-based guides if possible. The features and possibilities of the two media should be contrasted and compared. Key elements should be explored:

Sample work

● audience
● content
● structure
● appearance.

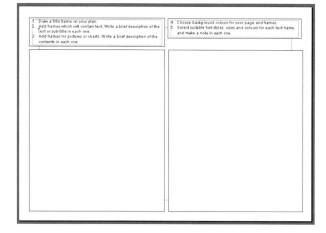

After critical discussion of these points, the class will need to decide what to include in their own guide. The guide should be divided into 8-10 pages to be created by small groups of children working collaboratively. Ensure that sufficient breadth of study is included. Aspects to cover might include:

● Industry and employment
● Transport
● Housing
● Commerce and retail
● Leisure
● Education
● Religion
● Health care
● Law and order
● National events such as war, plague, invasion, settlement, technological advances.

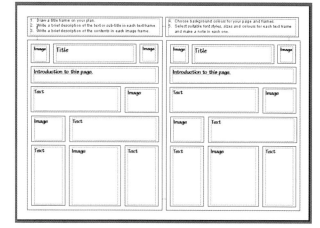

A home page or introduction should also be included, although this may be better left until the content is complete. It could be provided as an extension activity or created by the teacher in collaboration with the whole class.

Sample work

2. It may be sensible to create a template for the individual web pages in the light of class discussion. This would make the activity accessible to younger and/or less able pupils.

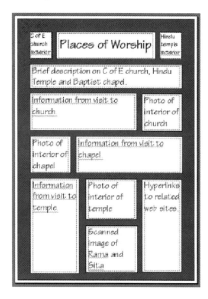

Planning is probably the most important part of this activity and should be thoroughly explained to the children before they start. A planning sheet could be provided, with sections to focus the children's thoughts on the main points of consideration.

Children can work on screen or paper, depending on the resources available and other learning objectives. They should produce a detailed plan, which should be approved before they start to collect materials.

From this plan, the group should make a list of information and images they need and distribute the tasks amongst them.

3. Sources of the information needed should also be listed. They may need to go out into the town, refer to information gathered during visits, use scanners or digital cameras, search the Internet or CD-ROMs or interview local people. This will take some organisation and should be set within strict time limits to prevent this stage from prolonging the overall activity.

It may be helpful to give them a limited range of resources to search through. Leaflets and guides can be provided, as can web addresses of useful sites and a collection of photographs of the local area.

When collecting and editing text, care should be taken to include the use of correct historical vocabulary relating to time and dates, characteristics of periods of history and reasons for and results of historical events.

Some ICT techniques may need to be taught beforehand, although most of those needed should have been developed during previous years:
- Searching the Internet or a CD-ROM for information and images
- Using a digital camera
- Using a scanner
- Word processing text.

4. Once the resources and information have been collected the production of the web page can begin. Children do not have to use web publishing software to produce these pages, although it is relatively easy to use. Many word processors, desktop publishing and multimedia authoring packages allow you to create web pages. All the children should use the same software to make the final combining of the pages simple and quick.

All the resources, both text and images, should be prepared and saved in one place. They can then be copied and pasted into the frames created on the web page or directly onto the page. This may need to be demonstrated by the teacher, but should have been covered before. Most of the skills needed to complete the web page will have been learned whilst using a word processor and multimedia authoring software.

Perhaps the only new skill will involve inserting hyperlinks to other useful web pages. This can usually be done simply by typing the URL of the appropriate web site. Most recent software will automatically insert a hyperlink from the text. Again this technique will need to be demonstrated by the teacher. Ideally a data projector will be used, however a large monitor or TV can be used instead.

Children's work

NC History KS2

Pupils will learn and apply a range of geographical skills described in Attainment Targets 1-5 of the National Curriculum.
Pupils should be taught:
7 A study investigating how an aspect in the local area has changed over a long period of time, or how the locality was affected by a significant national or local event or development or by the work of a significant individual.

Planning

These activities form part of KS2 work in History on carrying out a local history study. They also cover KS2 work in English on writing non-fiction for different audiences. The on-screen work will also help to develop the children's ICT skills. Word processing and multimedia authoring skills will be developed during these activities.

The activities use text and image entry and formatting techniques within a web publishing package. Children will need to be taught how to collect and save resources before using them in the publication. The additional use of sound and video files would require the application of skills developed through working with images.

Differentiated activities can be provided through the preparation of a basic structure for some children or additional support where appropriate. Differentiation can also be achieved through the expectations of the outcome; some groups' work may have a simpler structure or use less text.

Management

Children need access to web publishing software such as **FrontPage** or **Dreamweaver**, although a similar result could be produced using the web design features of a word processor or DTP package.

This activity is best carried out with children working in pairs or small groups. Some may benefit from adult support. Discussion and collaboration should be encouraged throughout. The groups are effectively producing a web site which can be viewed by a world-wide audience and should be aware of the responsibility to accuracy that this carries with it.

Teaching and learning

Teaching

The teacher introduces the concept of paper and web-based local history guides. The main features should be discussed, along with the need for a clear structure and a content carefully designed for the target audience. Emphasis should be placed on detailed planning and coherent structure rather than busy pages and special effects.

The children can design their web pages on screen or on paper, but they will need to be familiar with the capabilities of the software to allow them to include them in their plans. The evaluation of products by the target audience forms an important part of the process. Other children, parents and other adults may be involved at various stages of the project. Pupils should be encouraged to take their opinions into consideration when developing their work.

Assessment

This activity provides opportunities for assessment in History, English and ICT. In particular chronological understanding, knowledge and understanding of events, people and changes in the past, historical interpretation, historical enquiry, organisation and communication, local history study, non-fiction writing for a given audience, collaboration and web publishing skills can be monitored and assessed. Children may also be involved in research to identify what is needed in the web pages and to collect resources to be used in the work.

Formative assessment will take place throughout the activity, particularly through intervention during independent work and discussion during whole class sections. The final product will provide evidence of the knowledge and skills which have been developed during the activity. The work can be printed out in book form to be used, perhaps by a more limited audience from the online pages.

Children's work

Teaching and learning

Techniques used by teacher

■ Finding and providing resources
■ Uploading a web site

Techniques used by children

■ Deciding on the content
■ Creating a structure
■ Entering and formatting text, images, videos and sounds
■ Controlling the transitions between events
■ Linking pages and events

Sample activity

KS2 Geography

Local Study

Aim

To carry out a geographical study of the local area and exchange the data collected with a school in a contrasting location.

Setting the scene

Places change and develop over time. By gathering information about a locality and comparing it with a contrasting area, similarities, differences and patterns can be identified. Information can be gathered from many sources and communicated in a variety of forms. This data must be accurate and up to date and can be exchanged with people in a different area or country.

Activity

You are going to find out about the place where you live, investigating what it is like now and how it has developed. You will need to collect information and present it clearly and accurately. You can exchange information with children in another school so that you can discover what is the same and what is different about their area.

1. Discuss what you know about the place where you live. You will all have a lot of information to share with the class. It might help to organise it into sections:
   - What kind of settlement is it?
     - city
     - town
     - village
   - Where is it within the country?
     - county
     - region
   - What is the landscape like?
     - flat
     - hilly
     - mountainous
   - What is the weather/climate like?
     - dry
     - wet
     - windy
     - warm
     - cold
   - What are the houses like?
     - old
     - new
     - close together
     - spread out
     - terraced
     - semi-detached
     - detached
     - flats
   - What kind of jobs do people have?
     - services
     - manufacturing
     - agricultural
     - transport

- What facilities are provided?
  - entertainment
  - health
  - retail
  - transport

2. You are going to find out why the place is like it is. You will need to collect information by visiting local places, using paper-based materials and using CD-ROMs and the Internet. You will carry out surveys, make measurements and examine maps and written information.
   - Use a database to find out about the types of homes people live in. Carry out a survey of housing in different areas of the village, town or city. Find out whether housing changes as you get further from the centre. Suggest reasons for your findings and illustrate them.
   - Use maps to find out what land is used for in your area, for example housing, transport, retail, manufacturing, public services and leisure. Colour these on a map so that you can see how much of the area is taken up by each. Do the same thing using maps from 100 and 200 years ago. Suggest reasons for any changes you can see.
   - Collect weather data for one month and enter it into a spreadsheet. Predict patterns in the weather related to seasonal change, rainfall, temperature and wind speed. Produce graphs to prove or disprove your theories. Suggest ways in which the weather in your area affects the lives of people who live there.
   - Identify a recent development in your area, perhaps a new road or the building of a new supermarket. Find out how it has affected the local environment and the lives of people in the area. You could carry out surveys of traffic, noise levels, pollution and wildlife.

3. Send your information by email to children in a different area. You will need to make sure that you have checked it carefully. Use a word processor to write about what you were trying to find out, how you collected information and what you learned. You can send word processing, database, spreadsheet and image files that you have created and used during your investigation.

You will receive information about the area where the other children live. You can email each other with any further questions.

Children's work
Geography Activity

1. Whole class work

   Discuss what the children already know about the place where they live. Focus on geographical facts rather than opinions. A series of questions may help to do this: these could be projected onto a screen or interactive whiteboard using a data projector. This would enable you to use a word processor to capture the children's ideas.

   The focus of the discussion should be the human and physical geographical features of the area. The size, type and location of the settlement needs to be established before exploring the reasons why it developed and the ways in which it has changed and is changing.

   Ask the children what else they could find out about the location and how they could go about this. The importance of primary sources of evidence should be emphasised. Children should be given opportunities to explore the local area and gather data and information. The need for accuracy should be explained and suitable methods used.

   Explain that the information gathered will help them to understand the place where they live and will be shared with children in another part of the country. This link needs to have been arranged with the class teacher well in advance. Email addresses need to be exchanged and information, such as the available software, project content and probable activities, agreed. Decisions will need to be made about whether children communicate individually or as a class. If this is the first time the class has used email, it is simpler to use one address to exchange data and send messages. Individual pen pal relationships may develop from this and be used in future projects.

2. Independent work

   There are many aspects of the data collection and processing which can be carried out more efficiently using ICT. Here are a few examples:

   ● An electronic database can be used to determine a relationship between two sets of data, e.g. type of house and distance from town centre. It can also be used to create graphs an charts quickly and accurately. The interpretation of these graphs can then be the main focus of the lesson, rather than their production. The children should start with a problem to solve, hypothesis to prove or question to answer. The

Photographs of different types of houses can be taken with a digital camera.

data collection and processing should then be carried out appropriately.

● Different types and ages of map can be found on the Internet or CD-ROM for any locality. This enables children to make comparisons and learn about changes and developments. There are advantages to using these maps alongside rather than instead of paper-based resources. An Ordnance Survey map will cover a greater area and can be used outside the classroom.

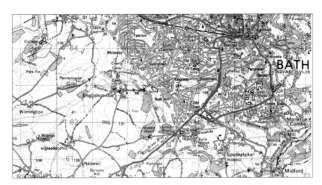

Different types of map can be found on the Internet or CD-ROM for any locality.

● Weather data can be collected using data logging equipment. This allows continuous data to be collected accurately. This can be entered into a spreadsheet which can be used to identify patterns and calculate averages and totals. Accurate graphs and charts can be produced quickly. This allows children to concentrate on the interpretation of the data, rather than the production of graphs. The

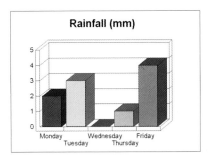

Database and graphing software can be used to produce suitable graphs of various types of information and data.

Children's work

Geography Activity

children should start with a problem to solve, hypothesis to prove or question to answer. The data collection and processing should then be carried out appropriately.

- Information about a recent local development can be accessed via local newspaper reports. These are often available on CD-ROM or archived on the Internet. Local Government web sites may contain information about the planning process and the effects on the local environment.

3. Group work

The information gathered and processed can be presented using a word processor or desktop publishing software, it could equally be combined with handwritten materials. The advantages of using electronic media include the easy combination of charts, table, images and text within one document. This can then be

exchanged, via email, with another school and used to compare localities. This could develop into a longer term project covering two units of work, a local study and a contrasting locality. The email link could also be used to develop other work, such as collaborative writing or web site creation.

The teacher will need to establish a link with another appropriate school and check that data is sent in a usable format. There are many projects, some with funding, currently running to encourage this type of activity. Details can be obtained from the BECTa and NGfL web sites.

ICT Techniques

- Sending text and images via email

Children's work

Teaching and learning

NC Geography KS2

Pupils will learn and apply a range of geographical skills described in Attainment Targets 1-5 of the National Curriculum.

6a pupils should be taught the knowledge, skills and understanding through the study of a locality in the United Kingdom

7a study at a range of scales – local, regional and national

7b study a range of places and environments in different parts of the world, including the United Kingdom and the European Union

7c carry out fieldwork investigations outside the classroom

Planning

These activities form part of KS2 work in Geography on carrying out a local study and study of a contrasting locality. They also cover KS2 work in English on writing non-fiction for different audiences. The on-screen work will also help to develop the children's ICT skills. Word processing, data handling

and email skills will be developed through these activities.

The activities use data collection and interrogation techniques within databases and spreadsheets. Children will need to be taught how to collect data and organise data, structuring a database or spreadsheet to answer questions and prove hypotheses. This data is to be exchanged with children in another area. Children will needed to be taught how to send and receive emails and attachments and to use the information they receive. These skills are most effectively taught to the whole class using demonstration and short practical tasks.

Differentiated activities can be provided through the preparation of a basic structure for some children or additional support where appropriate. It is likely that children's language and mathematical capability may affect their engagement with these activities. Differentiation can also be achieved through the expectations of the outcome; some groups' work may have a simpler structure or investigate less complex issues.

Children's work

Management

It is essential that teachers from the two schools involved are able to plan carefully together to ensure that the information exchanged is usable by both groups of children. The email connection will need to be reliable and software compatible. Most schools use *Outlook Express* (Microsoft) or *Netscape Messenger* (Netscape) for email access. Neither of these will cause compatibility problems, but it is advisable to test the system by sending a few messages and attachments to ensure that all files can be opened and used. The data handling software needs to be similar and compatible.

Children need access to data handling software such as
- *Information Workshop* (Black Cat)
- *Junior Pinpoint* (Longman Logotron)
- *Excel* (Microsoft)
- *Number Magic* (RM)
- *Number Box* (Black Cat)
- *Counter* (Black Cat)
- *Starting Graph* (RM)

This activity is best carried out with children working in pairs or small groups. Some may benefit from adult support. Discussion and collaboration should be encouraged throughout. The groups are producing information which will be shared with other class members and children in another school. The importance of accuracy and clear presentation should be emphasised.

Teaching

The teacher introduces the concept of carrying out a geographical investigation of the local area. The work should start from what the children know already.

Teaching and learning

Methods of further study can then be explored with the children being made aware of the purpose and audience of the work.

The children can carry out data collection work on screen or on paper, but it will be most efficient to use software to sort, interrogate and present the information. Some skills may need to be taught to allow them to make the most of the software's features.

The children should be familiar with the use of email, but sending and receiving attachments may need to be covered. The method of communication and audience for the work should be clear from the start of the work.

Assessment

This activity provides opportunities for assessment in Geography, Maths, English and ICT. In particular geographical enquiry, knowledge and understanding of places, knowledge and understanding of patterns and processes, knowledge and understanding of environmental change and sustainable development, non-fiction writing for a given audience, collaboration, communication and data handling skills can be monitored and assessed.

Formative assessment will take place throughout the activity, particularly through intervention during independent work and discussion during whole class sessions. The final products will provide evidence of the knowledge and skills which have been developed during the activity. The work can be printed out as well as being exchanged electronically. It may be used to form part of a class book or web site.

Techniques used by teacher

- Send and receive email
- Send and receive attachments

Techniques used by children

- Send and receive email
- Send and receive attachments
- Collect and organise information in a suitable form for emailing
- Data collection, interrogation and presentation

Techniques checklist

This chart provides a checklist of the knowledge, understanding and techniques that relate to using ICT for exchanging and sharing information

Section 1: Introduction to exchanging and sharing information

● *Know about the types of ICT activities described in the book*	Book aims	1
● *Understand the ways in which ICT can be used to help to produce resources*	Compose, modify and design	1
● *Understand the advantages of using the multimedia features of ICT*	The value of ICT	1
● *Know about the ways in which ICT can be used to create flexible, differentiated resources*	Be your own publisher	1
● *Know about the multimedia features of ICT*	The power of multimedia	2
● *Know about the range of software which facilitates the creation of multimedia resources*	Multimedia authoring programs	2
● *Know about software which facilitates the production of multimedia presentations*	Presentation software	3
● *Know about software which can create websites incorporating multimedia features*	Web publishing software	3
● *Know about the software which can be used to communicate using email*	Email	3
● *Know when to use a word processor and when to use multimedia authoring programs*	Other generic programs	3
● *Understand how a range of software can be used and combined to create resources*	Linking ICT	3
● *Know about the variety of ways in which children can be organised when using ICT*	Ways of working	4
● *Understand the advantages and disadvantages associated with individual work using ICT*	Individual work	4
● *Understand the advantages and disadvantages associated with group work using ICT*	Group work	4
● *Understand the advantages and disadvantages associated with whole class teaching using ICT*	Whole class teaching	4
● *Know about the ways in which ICT can support teachers and children in developing and communicating ideas*	Developing and communicating ideas	5
● *Know about exchanging and sharing information within the NC subject orders*	NC subject orders	5
● *Know about exchanging and sharing information within the NC ICT subject orders*	NC orders for ICT	5
● *Know about the standards of ICT competence for teachers*	ICT standards for teachers	5

Section 2: Planning

● *Know how to plan a multimedia presentation or web site*	How it works	6
● *Know how to plan the content of your presentation or web site*	Deciding on the content	6
● *Know how to plan pages or slides in a presentation or web site*	Creating a structure	7
● *Know how to choose suitable software for your first multimedia publication*	Starting from scratch	8
● *How to start creating a presentation*	Creating a new presentation	8
● *How to choose the right layout*	Choosing a layout	8
● *How to enter text into the layout*	Adding text	9
● *How to change the size of the frames*	Changing frames	9

Section 5: Presenting and sharing

Section 6 Teaching and learning with ICT

Glossary

Browser: software which allows you to search through information or files /17

Bullet point: a mark to show one item in a list /6

CD-ROM: a CD containing multimedia information which can be accessed but not altered /6

Clip art: line drawings or other simple drawings saved as files /17

Custom animation: visual and sound effects added to text and images /10

Dialogue box: a box which appears on the screen to allow you make decisions /17

Digital camera: a camera that takes photos in digital form /3, 20

Downloaded: saved onto a computer from another source, e.g. the Internet or a CD-ROM /17

Email address: the address used to send a message to a person's email account /23

File handling: the ability to create folders, locate and move files around within a filing structure /12

Font style: the size and style of text /15

Formatting tools: a set of tools used to alter the appearance of text and images /12

Generic program: a program that does not have its own subject content so that you can use it to create your own work /3

Graduated colour: smooth transition from one colour to another /13

Hierarchical structure: a structure in which information is organised into sections which can be explored as the user wishes /7

Hot spots: a link between different marked places in a document or between documents /32, 34

Hyperlink: a link between different marked places in a document or between documents /7, 32, 34

Justify: to line up text along the left or right margin, with spacing between the words adjusted /15

Linear structure: a structure in which events happen in a predetermined order in sequence /7

Midi files: type of sound file usually associated with music clips /27

Motion clips: video or animated clips /26

MP3: recent format of sound file which takes up very small amounts of memory /27

Multimedia package: software that can show sound, images, text, video and animation with buttons to link different resources /6

Navigation: the method by which you view and move around information /30

Navigation view: screen which shows the way in which pages are linked together /36

Notes Page View: view in which presenter's notes can be written /11

Outline View: view in which the text can be seen and edited /11

Picture or image toolbar: the toolbar used to edit pictures and images /20

Presentation: an electronic slide show /6

Presentation software: software that combines text, images and sound in an electronic slide show /12

Preview: run a presentation or multimedia resource as it will be seen by the audience /26

Publish: save in a form that can be run on a computer without the software installed /35

Scale to fit: applied to images to avoid distortion and keep the proportions of the image the same regardless of size /26

Scanner: a copier that captures pictures in digital form that can be used in a computer /3, 20

Scrollbar: the side bar tool to move through a document /10, 11

Search engine: a website which facilitates searches for information on a given subject /20

Slide: one page within a presentation /8

Slide Show: view in which slide show is actively running and cannot be edited /10, 11

Slide Sorter View: view in which the order of the slides can be altered /11

Slide View: view in which the whole slide can be seen and edited /11

Template: a page design provided as part of the program /13

Text frame: an editable box you can type text in /15

Texture: a background image giving the effect of a texturised surface /13

Thumbnail: a miniature version of an image /36

Toolbar: a set of buttons with screen commands /15

Transitions: the visual effect used to move from one page to another /30

Undo: a tool to go back to a previous situation /20

Uploading: publishing a web site on the Internet /30, 35

URL: Uniform Resource Locator or web address /34

Video frame: a frame drawn on the screen in which a video clip or animation can be placed /26

Video Properties dialogue box: a dialogue box which allows you to control the appearance and timing of a video or animated clip /26

Wav files: type of sound file usually associated with sound effects /27

Web publishing software: software that can be used to create web pages and manage websites /12

Web site: a series of linked pages of information on the Internet /6

Wizard: a process in which you answer a sequence of questions in order to produce a document /8

Word-processing: writing, editing and designing text /12